Talking #browntv

Talking #browntv

Latinas and Latinos on the Screen

Frederick Luis Aldama and
William Anthony Nericcio

THE OHIO STATE UNIVERSITY PRESS

COLUMBUS

Library of Congress Cataloging-in-Publication Data is available online at catalog.loc.
gov.

Cover design by Angela Moody
Text design by Juliet Williams
Type set in Adobe Palatino

♾ The paper used in this publication meets the minimum requirements of the American
National Standard for Information Sciences—Permanence of Paper for Printed Library
Materials. ANSI Z39.48-1992.

To our next-gen Latinxs,
who continue the struggle
of *la multimediated causa*

CONTENTS

Introduction   From Black and White to Shades of #browntv   1

Section I   Toward a Theory of a Brown Televisual Imaginary   7

Section II   *Pinche* Paradoxes   25

Section III   *Sombreros* to *Pistoleros*   52

Section IV   From *Niños* and Teens to *Comidas*   89

Section V   Fear, Loathing, and the Latinx Threat   110

Coda   The Brown Revolution *Will* Be Televised   132

Notes   157

Bibliography   163

Index   175

From Black and White to Shades of #browntv

Adjust your TV sets—and all other multimedia paraphernalia. Our book sets out to add to and complicate the picture image we have of the US. After a long history of struggle, we've gone from black and white to Technicolor.

Today, we're seeing more and more shades of browns and other colors in TV. Our book seeks to tease out and make luminous the presence of that color we call brown. We will cover all variety of TV (with some nods to film) representations of Latinxs, beginning with masked *vaqueros*, winding our way through Saturday-morning cartoons, sitcoms, today's comic book superhero webisodes along with border-patrol reality TV and ending with multimediatized porn. In a way, the book is a kind of how-to-manual for all of us to be able to adjust our dials to *see* clearly how the multi-spectrumed shades of brown appear in the history of US TV production and consumption; and, sadly, how they don't appear.

The book responds to an urgent moment in our *multimediated* history—screens, screens everywhere, and not a thought to think (or, perhaps better, too too much to see, reason subjected and enslaved to an optical ubiquity with racialized/racializing DNA).

Today we are the majority minority in the US. We number upward of fifty-one million on the 2010 US census plus twelve million undocumented. Contrast this with just a few decades ago when our numbers were in the middle teens: 14.6 million in 1980. Some have identified this as the *Latinization* of the US (see Jorge Ramos's *The Latino Wave*, for instance); others like ourselves call it a Browning of America, claiming the term *brown* as our own. And it's happening right before our very eyes. Take a look at playgrounds not just in historically dominant Latinx areas of the Southwest but in those regions like the Midwest, and you'll see names like Mandujano, Díaz, Ramirez, and the like on school rosters—you'll see phenotypic shades of brown pattern otherwise all-white school assemblies.

But this doesn't mean it's time to get the popcorn out. While our demographic weight in this country is immense, we still bump up against robust ceilings of oppression. What was once hypervisible in deeply reactionary regions like Arizona and Alabama, with their history of imposing laws that curtailed the freedom of Latinxs, is now commonplace throughout the US. There's the trumped-up fear that the Browning of America will do just that—turn the US into a place that looks and sounds more like Latin America. There's the fear that we're the ones taking the jobs—and all else, leaving nothing for the white guy. This is far from the case, of course, but there you have the power of the media—a media that can and does influence the way people perceive, think, feel, and act in the world.

Those racist Arpaio gunslingers and underhanded legislators like those in Arizona of yesteryear are today coming out of the woodwork everywhere. The result: the fracturing of our *familias* and communities; the fleeing of our brothers and sisters across borders.

We thought Sergio Arau's *A Day Without a Mexican* (2004) was a mockumentary. Well, it's not. Our streets are empty. Our restaurants are closing. Our fruit lies rotting. Today's media-flamed xenophobia has made us ghosts.

While our presence constitutes some of the main building blocks of the everyday reality in the US, we're not seen much in the *reel* world. TV in the US neglects (and sometimes purposefully so, as we'll discuss later in the book) the presence of Latinxs in this country. When mainstream TV creators and showrunners choose *not* to bring shades of brown into their stories, we cry foul. The lived reality of all in the US that is more and more brown-inflected increasingly stands in sharp contrast to the brownout that continues to be recreated in the media. We Latinxs go to the movies more than any other ethnic group in the US (see the Motion Picture Association of America's 2013 report), yet too often we're not in the movies we see. We watch more TV than any other group, yet we're staggeringly underrepresented, not well represented.

To pull out some numbers, since the 1950s, when we composed approximately 3 percent of the television population, we were down to a slim 1 to 1.6 percent throughout the 1980s and 1990s. Our numbers improved somewhat in the late 1990s, inching back up to only 3 percent of the TV viewing population. In 2015 Latinx characters made up 5.1 percent of speaking roles; most of the roles were as criminals, cops, and undocumented laborers. In 2016 the sum total of all ethnic and racial minorities represented in TV as characters came in at only 11.4 percent (see Isabel Molina-Guzmán). And this was not because of the good graces of the near all-white and all-male production, direction, creation of our TV imaginary. As Molina-Guzmán mentions, it was the result of "decades of work by activists in the Multi-Ethnic Media Coalition ma[king] the top five TV networks (ABC, CW, Fox, CBS, NBC) accountable for the lack of diversity in front of and behind the TV screen" (3). Put simply, Latinxs are 18 percent of the population, yet we are less than 3 percent represented on screens across the US. It's certainly not reflective of the majority racial and ethnic demographic makeup of the US (see the research of Dana E. Mastro and Elizabeth Behm-Morawitz).

At the same time, in this book we want to consider how we are also very present in TV—and possibly even more than before. Here we consider how we are present as identifiably Latinx in shows like *Cristela* (canceled in 2015[1]), sci-fi TV epics like *Caprica* (2010) and *Star Trek: Discovery* (2017–), independent webisodes like *East WillyB* (2013) alongside those created with bigger production dollars such as ABC's *Agents of S.H.I.E.L.D: Slingshot* (2016). We will also explore how #browntv presents Latinxs as safe: either as assimilated or with Anglos in Brownface and Brownvoice. The characters simply *are* Latina, just as others in these shows simply *are* Anglo. Of course, upon our second glance together we discover that there's more here than first meets the eye.

This book seeks to wander in and through the various ways we're represented in TV—ways that can and do conjure certain anxieties. Are we *really* fly-off-the-handle histrionic? Are we really only all body: as working arms or hypersexualized bodies? Are we really only American dreamers? Have we internalized values other than those of our parents and grandparents? Are we losing touch with our ancestral culture? Where do we find our *Latinidad*—our Latino-ness today? Has this changed in our browning of America, and if so, how do we re-regard mainstream culture with its central ingredients of TV? Does an *arrival* also mean our *erasure*?

What we are interested in is exploring in a free-flowing yet far-reaching way the many tensions and paradoxes that have enveloped the *recreation* of Latinxs in TV. We've chosen to write this book as a conversation, considering this an ideal format for presenting two distinctive voices (and with these, our differing experiences and knowledge) that seek to bring to light the contrapuntal interplay of the tensions and paradoxes that envelope our representation in TV pop cultural media.

We follow this introduction with five sections and a coda. They are as follows. Section I, "Toward a Theory of Brown Televisual Imaginary," considers how we might theorize our simultaneous presence (both on TV and as consumers of TV) and absence; we are minimally represented, and when we are represented it's in exaggerated, denigrative ways. In section II, "*Pinche* Paradoxes," we tease apart the ways that we are at once absent and present, as well as put under a microscope how those who have *made it* (Eva Longoria and Sofía Vergara, for instance) do little to complicate the #browntv landscape; indeed, we conclude that until we're truly postrace, #browntv constructions within and outside the Latinx community easily slip into Manichean reformulations. Section III, "*Sombreros* to *Pistoleros*," considers a number of different genres—from Westerns to zombies to sci-fi—that concretize the modern racialized consciousness of what it means televisually to be Latinx. Here, too, we are mindful of how Latinx subjects are not passive sponges. Rather, we demonstrate how we actively metabolize and reconstruct Latina/o-ness in and through such TV shows as *Wonder Woman* and films like *Blade Runner*. And we put gender under our Latinx lens to examine how bad and good are mapped uncritically onto dark- *and* light-skinned Latinx subjects. In section IV, "From Niños and Teens to Comidas," we move from characters on Saturday-morning cartoons like El Dorado in *The Super Friends* (1981) to films like Jerrod Hess's *Nacho Libre* (2006) that continue to etch deep lines of division between us and them. We find powerful antidotes to this in shows like *El Tigre* and the *Powerpuff Girls* that work at the level of content and form to dazzle and complicate what it means to be Latinx.

Our denouement happens in section V, "Fear, Loathing, and the Latinx Threat," which considers how TV shows like *Border Wars* (2010–2015), *Border Security: America's Frontline* (2016–), and *Homeland Security USA* (2009) construct a Latinx threat narrative, exploring how these shows reveal how what used to be considered only an Arizona problem (the SB 1070 "law" to justify carceral-state mechanisms that targeted our people) is now a national problem. We wrap it all up with the coda, "The Brown Revolution *Will* Be Televised," where we examine the liberating possibilities of Latinx-created erotica. We end with the reminder that the #browntv *reel* imaginary has consequences for the *real* lives of Latinxs, and that while our odyssey in the analysis of #browntv and Latino/a pop culture generally is important, it is really the boots-on-the-ground mobilization that will ultimately realize the moment when #browntv reflects our complex subjectivities and experiences. Our hope with this book is to create a varied and vibrant tapestry that interweaves the cultural, historical, and sociopolitical with various examples of how Latinx subjects have been #browntv *mediatized*.

This book seeks to extend the conversation and the interpretive terrain of the work of our colleagues across the country. They include Mary Beltrán (*Latina/o Stars in U.S. Eyes*), Isabel Molina-Guzmán (*Latinas and Latinos on TV*), Myra Mendible (*From Bananas to Buttocks*), Deborah Paredez (*Selenidad*), Angharad N. Valdivia (*Latina/os and the Media*), Frances Negrón Muntaner

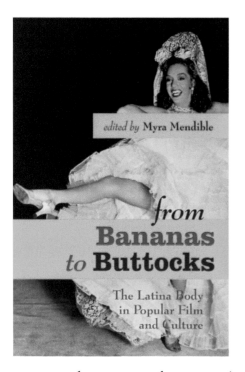

edited by Myra Mendible

from **Bananas** *to* **Buttocks**

The Latina Body in Popular Film and Culture

(*Boricua Pop*), Arlene Dávila (*Latinos, Inc.*), Charles Ramírez Berg (*Latino Images in Film*, among others), Frances Aparicio and Susana Chávez-Silverman (*Tropicalizations*), Richard T. Rodriguez (*Next of Kin*), Chon Noriega and Ana M. López (*The Ethnic Eye*), Rosa Linda Fregoso (*The Bronze Screen*), Camilla Fojas (*Border Bandits*), and Priscilla Ovalle (*Dance and the Hollywood Latina*). And, we see in all of these various approaches to Latinx representation in the media different methods used, from image to content analysis. Some analyze and evaluate whether the images of Latinxs are accurate or positive, breaking this down into subgroups including those formed by categories like gender and sexuality. Some analyze and also condemn destructive images of Latinxs such as in the oversexed Latina or violent gangbanger Latino stereotypes. Others select a group of programming to analyze, measuring the appearance of different image categories. Yet others compare demographic numbers with the appearance of Latinxs in the media. We do a little of all of the above in this book—and with semiotic and cognitive analysis thrown in.

Ultimately, we aim to push back against a representational landscape that's monochromatic white—and with white, middle-class norms. What better way to tell this story than as a conversation—a dramatic narrative that includes more than us but that reaches out to you as the reader to participate in this exploratory journey of Latinx life as it's *recreated* and *multimediated* in #browntv. Stay tuned: the revolution *may or not be* televised, but our debates and *desmadres* on Latinx bodies in mainstream media are, for sure, something necessary in the here and now.

SECTION I

Toward a Theory of a Brown Televisual Imaginary

Frederick Luis Aldama, aka Fede: We find ourselves increasingly mediated in varying degrees of complexity in TV—and, well, all varieties of media formats. We're living in a time when we might most forcefully ask, how are the multiple media formats being used to represent the many ways of being Latinx today?

William Anthony Nericcio, aka Bill: We are everywhere and we are nowhere—it is almost as if we are "no one" or "no body"—I am reminded here of Odysseus and the Cyclops: "Who are you," the Cyclops bellows (or just says; we have to take Homer and Odysseus's word for it). "No one" / "No body," the clever Odysseus retorts, so that when he plunges his fiery timber (calling Dr. Freud) into the lusty, lumbering Cyclops's single eye, the creature's howls to his compatriots, "Nobody is hurting me," "Nobody fucked me over," are met with utter incomprehension. Similarly, Latinas and Latinos are everywhere and we are nowhere. I don't know if it is a saving grace, but we kind of lead the way when it comes to the pornography industry.[1] But on network television, we are *Devious Maids* (2013–16), or we are, yet again, *George Lopez* (2002–7), his latest show for Spike TV, a sometimes-clever amalgam of *Curb Your Enthusiasm* and *Seinfeld.* Eva Longoria is back on television, post MA in Chicano/a Studies at CSU Northridge, with a telenovela where she once again plays a funny, clueless, femme fatale—think *I Love Lucy* (1951–57) with cleavage and an accent. In the meantime, Emmy-winning actress Sofía Vergara is still tearing it up as Gloria on *Modern Family* (2009–), still hot, still tits-akimbo, still hotly sexualized and still the spitting image of Lupe Velez from the last century.

Yikes, is it really this dark? I hope not. Readers need to know that I am a creature of nostalgia—I have this website, *The Tex{t}-Mex Galleryblog,* that archives my relationship with the bygone days of television. The glory days when Chicanas/os were all over the boob tube—that's me over there with Lynda Carter (aka Linda Jean Córdova Carter²) in a graphic I lifted off my website.

From 1975 to 1979, she flitted across my television in Laredo, Texas, as Wonder Woman. While my incipient heteronormative juices were kicked into overdrive, I was also tangentially aware (Was it *TV Guide*? Was it *Time* magazine?) not only that she was Wonder Woman (a DC Comic I collected) but that the actress was Latina: Mexican American, to be precise. This is NOT inconsequential—if Speedy Gonzales can be looked to as a positive embodiment of Latinicity in American mass culture by adolescent Americans,³ can you imagine how this statuesque figure of beauty and intelligence dented my imagination?

Fede: In our various other books, we make the case that we should all be watching *recreations* of US reality in all its shaded, colorful complexities. It seems simple, yet the ineptitude of our #browntv creators clearly shows it to be difficult. As you point out, there's a laziness even among those like Longoria and Vergara in the way we're reconstructed and mediated. Is this an internalized colonialism or the work of some smart Latinas in a capitalist system? Vergara pulls in about $18 million a year, and Longoria's right on her heels.

The infamous scene at the Emmy Awards ceremony where Sofía Vergara was paraded around on a pedestal as Bruce Rosenblum, chairman of the Academy of Television Arts & Sciences, shared the logistics for the Emmy selections[4]

Bill: It's apparent that being a smart Latina in a capitalist system means you *are* a colonizer, of a sort—this might be fodder for another book wherein I return to my roots as a Walter Rodney–adoring Marxist, but being a businessperson means not taking risks, it means making a profit in the next quarter, it means putting a smile on the face of a shareholder. Recreations of US reality in all its shaded, colorful complexity have not translated (by and large) into profit for entertainment CEOs, and so it just does not go there. In the last three years, I have been trying to launch a TV show called *Mextasy*—imagine a television vehicle that's a cross between an Anthony Bourdain travel/food show, John Berger's *Ways of Seeing,* James Burke's *Connections,* and Carlos Fuentes's *The Buried Mirror* series, with a wanna-be TV star Chicano from Laredo, Texas, as the mouthpiece.

You think academe is hard, you should try show business.

And, ultimately, that's what it is: a business. In my book *Tex[t]-Mex* I say something to the effect that you don't go to Hollywood when you want American Studies Association–style postmodern ethnography—you are not going to see Clifford Geertz, Renato Rosaldo, and Ruth Behar on TMZ (thank god!). Getting your foot in the door may mean necessarily closing it behind you—although Eva Longoria is trying (peek below as Eva fills the screen as a Mexican maid while working as an executive producer behind the scenes).

For *Mextasy*, I had to go to NATPE (think MLA with spandex and cocaine), the National Association of Television Program Executives. It was there that I met Eva and asked her at a panel in 2015 why, instead of doing *Devious Maids*, she didn't do something like *Devious Neurobiology Professors*—it was good for a laugh from the audience and she was sweet and patient in her answer, which was "be patient" . . . "in time" . . . but you and I both know what that means.

Fede: I have a confession to make, Bill. I don't have cable TV—and I rarely have time to go to the movies. When I do watch shows, I'm plugged in to the blue-hazed digital spheres of my laptop or smartphone late at night when not even a mouse can be heard. At the end of the day I do consume TV, and a lot of it, but it's never synchronous (sometimes months or years after an original airtime), and it's never on a screen larger than thirteen inches.

I'm not alone. Nielsen ratings service tells us that there are forty-eight million Latinxs in the United States who watch TV.[5] And, of all the demographic groups that make up the US, Latinxs generally consume more TV than any other. That has to be a lot if you consider that the average person consumes around five hours of TV a day.

Bill: It is probably the fate of minority, working classes to give themselves over to the delights of escape and entertainment. We work so hard and for so little reward that the fleeting bouncing of photons on the magical boob tube is enough to placate the empty soul of a down-in-the-dumps laborer—think Gregor Samsa of Kafka's *Metamorphosis* infamy, or Willy Loman, from Arthur Miller's *Death of a Salesman,* and all I can imagine is my father sweating in Laredo's 110-degree summer heat. I remember well growing up at the side of my father's Sears lounge chair after work—he was a US postal clerk and would work long hours (some days even fourteen hours) on his feet channeling like Hermes all the communications flowing in and out of Laredo, Texas. Television was like manna from heaven or an opium bowl. Whether it was Mil Mascaras whipping the shit out of Wahoo McDaniel,

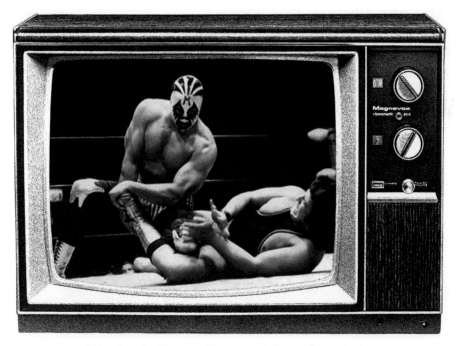

"TV in Laredo, Texas, or Mnemosyne's Scenes from a Lucha Libre." © Guillermo Nericcio García (2016).

Johnny Carson doing his fabled Carnac shtick, Raúl Velasco demurely introducing bosomy starlets or coolly touting a new telewonder (see below) on *Siempre en Domingo,*

or Red Foxx insulting his besieged son Lamont on *Sanford and Son,* the TV was an oasis away from worries—chores left undone, cruel nuns left behind at school, no mass to altar-boy at, and, best of all, no worrying about the future.

An aside: One memory stands out in particular: brought to mind with a chance encounter with Profe Ernesto Chavez's Instagram feed (funny how that works now).

It is Vikki Carr, aka Florencia Bisenta de Casillas-Martinez Cardona, born July 19, 1941, in El Paso, Texas. In the 1960s and '70s, she was a regular on *The Dean Martin Show* (1965–74), my dad's favorite show, and as Deano looked just like my beloved eccentric uncle Frank Nericcio (not only was there a

Dean Martin and Vicki Carr, from two episodes of *The Dean Martin Show*

resemblance, but they both sang and could both drink a distillery), my favorite show as well. But I didn't have a clue she was "Mexican" or "Tejana" or any of that ethnic studies stuff—she was just this beaming, beautiful soul making my dad and me laugh and smile. One of the shining stars of golden-age #browntv.

But that's just one side of the story—the shining stars that distracted us from our day-to-day lives. The other side is that for whatever reason, "Hispanics," as the Nielsens calls us—some mad confabulation that includes Chicanos from East LA, Tejanos from the Lower Rio Grande Valley, Boriqua from the mother islands or what's left of "Spanish" Harlem, Hispanos from New Mexico, Dominicans from Boston, and god knows what other constituencies, who would never party with each other let alone watch the same TV show (or, now, streaming media)—for whatever reason or reasons, we *devour* visual narrative: TV, movies, YouTube, you name it, we are on it like flies on caca.[6]

Fede: Is it that we are sucking at the opiate bowl, or are we as Latinxs in all our grand and glorious complexity metabolizing, digesting, and spitting back out something new from all that mainstream viscera? I don't mean a kind of *rasquachismo* at the margins, either. I mean are we as Latinx re-creators actively transforming the mainstream, in both our making and consuming practices? I'm thinking of the Asco art collective and Nuyorican Café as much as Robert Rodriguez's *Machete* series of films, his music video with Demi Lovato and Michelle Rodriguez, and his El Rey cable network shows. I'm thinking Cheech Marín's *Born in East LA* (1987) as much as the CW's *Jane the Virgin.* This is *rasquachismo* in action. It's also "color-conscious" TV-making, to use Molina-Guzmán's term to identify the creation of characters, in her words, "with ethnic and racial cultural and experiential specificity and thereby more complexity."[7]

Bill: Show business is show *business*—it is NOT a cauldron of innovation. Robert Rodriguez would make a complex case study. Where his first *Spy Kids* (2001) showcased a kind of progressive cinema (replete with embedded, subterranean positive semiotic glorifications of Latino culture), the *Machete* series, at times, takes a few steps back.

What is more stereotypical than a scary, violent, tattooed Mexican? From the so-called greaser films to *Treasure of the Sierra Madre* (1948) to *Machete* (2010), the archetype of the heterosexual, sexual predator Mexican has thrived—even as we type this, you and I are living through a nightmare fueled by this cinematic "Mexican" legacy: all of the tropes spewing out of neo-Nazi Donald Trump and friends' mouths were fueled by this trope-filled sequence.

These matters grow more and more complex and troublesome. With regard to Rodriguez, this is just the tip of the iceberg. Rose McGowan's early 2018 revelations regarding Rodriguez (and Quentin Tarantino), part of the Harvey Weinstein / #MeToo movement *escándalo*, are beyond nettlesome:

> In one of the memoir's most gripping chapters, she recounts her affair with director Robert Rodriguez (*Spy Kids, From Dusk till Dawn*), a smooth-talking, sensitive-seeming guy who turned out to be a Svengali. He and Quentin Tarantino were planning a double feature—*Planet Terror* and *Death Proof*—based on pulp movies of the 1970s, and he wanted McGowan to star. McGowan fell hard and fast, trusting Rodriguez enough to tell him about her experience with Weinstein. He proceeded to use the knowledge against her, she claims, as a tool

for mind games, starting with a scene in which Tarantino, playing a character in his movie, attacks McGowan's character. "I was in a backward world," she writes. "I was losing my grip on sanity." In what McGowan interpreted as the ultimate act of cruelty, Rodriguez "sold our film to my monster."[8]

It's hard not to see the neo-*machista* semiotics of *Machete* as mixed up with this matter—a kind of cinematic misogyny at the level of the unconscious that somehow works its way into the making of screened entertainment both on the screen and back in the trailers by the craft tables. Not to mention how closely these whispered disclosures take us back to the classic trope of the darkly sexual bandit of color.

Yikes!

Fede: I must say this news of Robert sideswiped me. After spending the day with Robert at his studios in Austin (I was finishing up *The Cinema of Robert Rodriguez*) I wasn't just smiling ear to ear as a fanboy. He was genuinely considerate of everybody circling the flame. Of course, being *nice* might be at the root of the problem we're seeing with the #MeToo movement. By this I mean that not only do those in power, and in a patriarchal society this would be *men* of all ethno-race backgrounds and sexual orientations, need a good slapping (and more), but that *nice* has led to a culture of complicity. Recently, I addressed the men in my hundred-plus-student "Film & Comics" course, telling them to buck up and speak out in support of their mothers, sisters, and female friends.

I'm not letting Robert or any other exploitive male (Latinx or otherwise) off the hook here, Bill. From McGowan's account, he was more than complicit. He used the information to exploit her. I'm deeply disappointed. From all the research I've done on him, he seemed genuinely interested in opening doors for women and Latinxs generally—and with no dirty strings attached. But perhaps I should have seen this subtextually. As you point out, there's a neo-*machista* semiotics that underlies his work that at once undermines and reinforces the kind of ugliness of mainstream media's reproduction of the virgin-versus-whore paradigm.

In my last breath here, however, let me mention briefly some of the semiotic subversions that he did realize. There's something remarkable about his ability to entertain *and* flip upside down preconceptions of Latinxs. With *Alita* (2019) Rodriguez entertains audiences with sci-fi Latinx warriors *and* he richly infuses his storyworld with hemispheric Latinx cultures and histories. (For more on this, see my "Robert Rodriguez's Fever-Dream: *Alita* and the Building of Latinx Sci-Fi Worlds.") I think of when Machete (Danny Trejo) uses a mop or a Weedwacker to combat the corrupt businessman Michael Booth's henchmen, Rodriguez invites us Latinx filmgoers in on the sociopolitically motivated gag: we *see* the mainstream stereotype (Latinx as only janitor or gardener), chuckle, and then see a serious history of how we Latinxs have powerfully reclaimed objects and spaces for resistance, mobilization, and sociopolitical transformation.

Bill: I hear you, *vato*—I feel you. I am just not sure that people always get it. Especially when we turn back to the substance of this book, which is #browntv. I can't help but feel that someone like "Julio" on *Sanford and Son* back in the day was having a bigger, more positive impact than *Machete* (and I like Danny Trejo, a lot, but semiotician *gotta speak the truth*). I was twelve years old when NBC's *Sanford and Son* (1972–77), starring Redd Foxx and Demond Wilson, "welcomed" Julio, a Puerto Rican rival junk dealer to their Los Angeles 'hood.[9] In its own subtle way, here we see what you just called the "metabolizing, digesting, and spitting back out something new." But again, maybe it is too subtle. Fred Sanford won't shake Julio's hand as he walks into his house with a goat—Sanford, too, blames Puerto Ricans for ruining Harlem by bringing in "Puerto Rican cockroaches."

But consider this—and this was the genius of Norman Lear's TV career in the seventies—that here we are watching prime-time TV and you've got an African American small business owner confronting a rival Puerto Rican small business owner living and working it all out in Los Angeles, California, where the show was set. That Lear adapted *Sanford and Son* and *All in the Family* (1971–79) for CBS from British shows (*Steptoe and Son*; 1962–1965; 1970–1974 as well as *Till Death Do Us Part*; 1965–1975) makes it even more complex (and international) in the end. And, for the moment, we will just leave out how the show introduces a Puerto Rican male lead set in a city like Los Angeles, a city with the highest density of Mexican Americans this side of Laredo and El Paso, Texas. I guess they could not find a Mexican in Los Angeles.

Fede: Is it just me, or does it seem like maybe we've taken some major steps back when it comes to today's browning of TV in America? When I watch prime-time shows with Latinxs from earlier epochs like the seventies I'm taken aback: they seem to take us places that TV doesn't dare to go today. You mention Julio on *Sanford and Son,* but of course there's *Chico and the Man* (1974–78). Freddie Prinze as Francisco "Chico" Rodriguez constantly foregrounded his Mexican and Hungarian ancestry in ways that you don't see in the *George Lopez* show or *Cristela,* for instance. In between his grumpy white boss's racist invectives, Chico would throw down some politically charged, satirical lines. When "The Man" makes a crack about Chico being Latino and therefore lazy, Chico responds by telling The Man how he got his Silver Star in Vietnam: "by *saving* the world from democracy." There are many other moments in *Chico and the Man* when Prinze dared to use caustic and socially pointed humor—and this was back in the mid-to-late 1970s. I used to watch *Chico* at my *abuelita*'s; she's the only one in the family who had a TV, so maybe this is also nostalgia speaking.

Bill: No, I think you are right, absolutely right. There was something going on back then that was subtle, but revolutionary. And you can find it going on even earlier in the sixties. Let's go back in time: it is May or June 1962, and as I frolic in my crib, six months old, at my house on Hendricks Avenue, things are happening at the Tivoli Theatre in downtown Laredo.

There, screening for the first time, is the latest animated short feature out of the genius hands of a crazy cohort of driven, twisted imagineers at Warner Bros. studios. Called "Mexican Boarders," directed by Friz Freleng, with Hawley Pratt, and written by John Dunn, the animated short tells the story of a visit to Speedy Gonzales by his cousin, Slowpoke Rodriguez.

I didn't get to see it until years later being used as afternoon filler by the local Laredo affiliate, but it needs to be front and center now.

I am writing about it here in our book because the episode throws a wrench (perhaps "heaves an ACME bomb" is better way of phrasing it; it *is* Warner Brothers cartoons I'm writing about) at a key chapter of my opus *Tex[t]-Mex,* chapter 3, which has the unfortunate distinction of sporting the longest title I've ever published: "Chapter Three. Autopsy of a Rat: Sundry Parables of Warner Brothers Studios, Jewish American Animators, Speedy Gonzales, Freddy López, and Other Chicano/Latino Marionettes Prancing about Our First World Visual Emporium; Parable Cameos by Jacques Derrida; and, a Dirty Joke."

What's remarkable about "Mexican Boarders" is the mise-en-scène, that old warhorse French term from film criticism that speaks to the setting, background, and tableau, if not the "actors" themselves. For in this 1962 classic, Speedy Gonzales is living the highlife in an upper-class Mexican town, "in the fine [bourgeois] hacienda of José Álvaro Meléndez." Most other Speedy shorts from the sixties feature Speedy and his cohorts living in trash ("Cannery Woe," 1961) or falling out of cantinas ("Tabasco Road," 1957)—and the bulk of my argument on Speedy, *Autopsy of a Rat,* focuses on this.

"Mexican Boarders" is different. Here, as you can see, Speedy lives the life of a *patrón,* in his "Casa de Gonzales."

This Speedy is what we call in Laredo, Texas, in our licentious and salacious patois, a high *sosiégate,* which literally means a *high calm-down,* and figuratively means "high get-over-your-own-damn-self" and sounds like "high society." So, this bougie *ratón* lives the good life, stealing cheese and such from Sylvester, who is so run down in "Mexican Boarders" that he has to resort to amphetamines to get him through his days.

That's when the key plot twist in this fable occurs and Speedy's country-mouse cousin, Slowpoke Rodriguez, arrives to visit—he is slow-talking, more heavily accented than Speedy (his voice provided not by Mel Blanc, Warner's heralded man of a thousand voices, but by Tom Holland).

All the sight gags in this awesome cinematic short revolve around Speedy saving his slow, country-bumpkin cousin from Sylvester owing to said bumpkin's obsessive-compulsive drive for more food—"Ahhmm steeeeel hawwww-wwwngreeee" becomes his Godot-like mantra. One particularly cool sight gag fuses the cubist sensibility of Georges Braque and Pablo Picasso.

But what is most striking about "Mexican Boarders" is the intellectual capacity of Slow-poke Rodriguez. Freleng et al. capitalize on his largely American audiences' expectations not only of a "Mexican" but of a rustic "peon" from the country—an urban/agricultural antagonism that transcends even nationalistic biases. For this slow-talking, slow-moving mouse is nobody's fool. Let him speak for himself: "maybe Slow-poke is pretty slow downstairs in the feet, but he is pretty fast upstairs in the *cabeza.*" Stopped by Speedy from emerging one evening to feed his ever-present appetite, Slowpoke demurs for a second, only to confess resignedly to his per-plexed cousin, "it's a far, far, better thing I do than if I starve."

Striking.

Freleng ventriloquizes his animated Mexican as a Sydney Carton–esque, Dickens-alluding literati; moreover, in the next scene, Rodriguez emerges as a Svengali-like mesmerist (no, I am not exaggerating!) who converts Sylvester into a fawning/fanning hypnotized lackey.

This ironic and surreptitious refiguration of the "Mexican" as cunning, mesmerizing subject—not to mention the Machiavellian potentiality embedded in this animated marionette—will have to be documented in the likely never-to-be-released second edition of *Tex[t]-Mex*.

Fede: Every year I teach Speedy-*squared*: the show *and* your work on the brown *queso*-eater and his compadres. Every year, the students (mostly Latinx) seem to get less and less the complexity of his creation—at least the creations seen in the episodes you mention. They don't get, too, the subversions in Adam de la Peña's flash-animation, *Minoriteam* (2005–6).

They *read* them straight, like they seem to do with much other layered (parodic, satiric, or otherwise) material. They need more and more a guide to show them *how* to read complexity. I wonder, is this because we have more Latinx content in TV and therefore they don't grow up like us having to *sleuth* out brown complexity, leaving no stone unturned? Maybe we should be more anxious about our so-called arrival in the mainstream. Yes, we're more present in cartoons, TV, and films, but in ways that serve up messages in simple and simple-minded ways—and this during a time purported to be *the* most creative in TV-making history.

Bill: It is going to get to the point where we will yearn for what we once, perhaps stupidly, reviled—new criticism. I can see myself craving even the most basic new critical close reading from my undergraduates. I think the key is to go with the flow and, somehow, also get in their faces. I think we're going to have to up our game. If I'm right about what I call the age of *Eyegiene* or *Eyegasm,* we are going to have to adapt our tools and skill set for a generation of visual consumers coming of age through smartphones—how can you deconstruct the virtual if the virtual is the air they breathe, viz. *Pokemon Go!* I think the trick will be to invade the media—it's dated now but remember Pop-up Video on VH1 . . . we have to do something like that, but make it work on smartphones. Something like this:

Fede: We loved our MTV, and now we, Latinxs especially, love our TV. And with modes of televisual consumption shrinking by the day (I carry my #browntv in my back pocket), we consume shows at all hours of the day. Indeed, on average Latinxs consume over five hours a day of #browntv. And we're the largest demographic to be chomping the popped corn in cinemas. We were the majority viewers of Justin Lin's *Fast & Furious* in 2009, a film that grossed more than $116 million within the first 10 days of its release (*Daily Variety,* "Film Box Office Wrap for the Weekend of April 10–12") and we filled those silver-screen seats with Lin's *Star Trek Beyond* (2016), which features an out-Asian Sulu (John Cho) and our very own Blatina Zoe Saldana as Lieutenant Nyota Uhura. Our familias on both sides of the US–Mexico border rocketed Pixar's *Coco* (2017) into the stratosphere; we just made history in Mexico with *Coco* earning the most of any film in Mexico's film history and $117,205,690 in its first three weeks of US release.[10]

Bill: Is this my cue to go Nietzsche on your ass, like some mexy Jeremiah, to chide that this addiction to the vicarious might just be some mass coping mechanism to counter the sadness of being an invisible people politically, an invisible (if growing) constituency in Hollywood and the ivory tower? Truth be told, I am never quite hopeless, just a tad fatigued with it all. We are writing this book during the greatest outbreak of anti-Mexican, anti-Latino sentiment for decades, maybe since the last *bracero* exile took place.

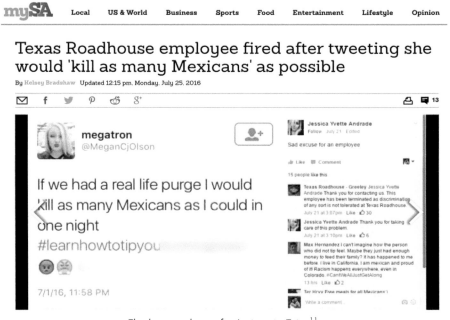

The here and now for Latinxs in Tejas[11]

So, we consume, consume, consume, from a mass media that increasingly finds us the focus/target of invective and rage—I have taken to using the hashtag #neokristallnacht on social media to underscore what I view to be a significant and dangerous backlash against multiculturalism: #Blacklivesmatter and #neokristallnacht as the signs of our times.

Maybe it's time for us to get into our time machine and think and talk about #browntv stars from the past—nostalgia a salve of sorts as we find our way and maintain our bearings.

The first Latino I remember seeing on TV was Manolito on *The High Chapparal* (NBC, 1967)! The actor's name turns out to be Henry Darrow—but that too, was a cipher.

From an interview with Darrow:

PARKE: When and why did you change your name from Enrique Delgado to Henry Darrow?

DARROW: "Delgado" did Latins. I had an agent named Carlos Alvarado and he only got scripts that had Latin parts. During the sixties and seventies there were lots of Latin parts floating around, and that's all I ever did. I played a non-Latin once, in a TV show with Victor Jory, and the character's name was Blackie; that was it.[12]

Fede: The mainstream whitens Latinxs (as you so deftly explore in *Te[x]t-Mex*). And, it continues to privilege whites in Brownface over actual Latinxs playing Latinxs.

#browntv makes us at once exotic *and* safe. It's this paradox that plagues mainstream's lazy manufacturings of Latinxs. We're at once present and then absent in our presence. We are absent, but then present in our absence. I don't want to leave you hanging, but let's swing the paradox of real and *reel* Latinxs into the next section of our *libro*: "*Pinche* Paradoxes."

SECTION II

Pinche Paradoxes

Fede: As we mentioned already, today our demographic numbers are more than abundant, yet we're still only a blip on the representational radar. And, when our high-frequency electromagnetic waves are detected, it's as a sign wrangled from its referent. I think what we might be beginning to carve out here is this sense that we are at once *really* here and yet *reely* not here. We exist in a state of being present and yet absent in our presence.

Bill: I think I know what you're getting at—the veritable elephant in the room—especially the here and now of the Trump administration and the rearing of the ugly hydra of popular fascism fueled by alt-right anti-Mexican race hate. How does a country that is demographically bursting with Mexicans, Dominicans, Puerto Ricans, and, now, spectacular blendings of all of the above, evolve in such a way that its popular entertainment machines, the infamous American culture industry, ignores that trace? Were I to revert back to my Chicano *movimiento* logic beginnings, I might say that there is a conspiracy afoot—and this is no knock on Chicano/a modes of interrogation, as the paranoia was merited and encouraged by political circumstances and entertainment industry practices.

As a kid, I remember fantasizing about fictional characters with Mexican accents on *Gilligan's Island* (1964–67) and *Lost in Space* (1965–68)—or maybe, those were just dreams of what we would call now, aping Lacan, the Brown Imaginary. As you know, I play with pictures much more than I write essays these days—case in point here:

I wonder if these mashups, here fused (or confused) contemporaries, Gilligan et al. *y El chapulin colorado* (1972–81) are just uncontrolled synaptic reactions to the divorce in my childhood between Laredo, Texas, at that time

"Psychotropic Bordered Memoir (with Gilligan y El Chapulin Colorado),"
Guillermo Nericcio García, digital mixed media (2017)

probably 99 percent Mexican American, and my suffusion in NBC/CBS television, where even just a glimpse of a Speedy Gonzales was enough to make me apoplectic with joy.[1]

Fede: Dreaming from slivers of brown worlds, Bill, is the exercising of our counterfactual capacity to extrapolate from our present (and past) and imagine a different tomorrow. As Latinxs we did this yesterday and we're doing this today. We did this with Speedy and his cousin, Slowpoke Rodriguez. We did this when the single Lucy takes a cruise ship to hunt for a man in a reconstructed La Havana, Cuba, where men are either sleeping or pimping their wares; she, of course, solves the threat of spinsterhood by hooking up with Ricky Ricardo, preternaturally talented at dancing, singing, and drumming the bongo.

We did this even with Orson Welles's violent sociopaths: the *familia* Grandi and their attack of the lily-white Susie (Janet Leigh) in *Touch of Evil* (1958).

And, aren't we forced to continue this creating of a Brown Imaginary even with Latina-produced TV shows like Eva Longoria's *Devious Maids.* In addition to distilling then reconstructing ourselves from all those constructions of Latinx subjects as bad, we do this with those that the mainstream spins as good and redemptive: Lou Diamond Phillips as Angel Guzman in *Stand and Deliver* (1988) or Esai Morales as Bob Morales in *La Bamba* (1987) and more recently as the ruthless Mexican kingpin Camino Del Rio in Netflix's *Ozark* (2017–); notably, the show (its showrunners are Christ Mundy and Bill Dubuque) writes in a character that's even more *bad* than Del: the white-trash kingpin Jacob Snell (Scottish Peter Mullen as Ozark trash?).[2] Only in the US could white trash be more *bad* than a Latino, right.

We're force-fed, Bill. But don't we metastasize this garbage and make it our own?

Bill: 'Tis true, 'tis so true. And those "Latino" classics, oft-times featuring actors, like Lou Diamond Phillips, aka "Young Mr. Upchurch,"[3] are the epitome of the what the late, oft-cited guru Jean Baudrillard termed the simulacra, a construction without autochthonous origin, or what the less-cited (and more evocative) Severo Sarduy pictured as camouflage (and even entomological metamorphosis, viz. caterpillars/butterflies)—peculiar and evocative shape-shiftings that proxy for the real, living, breathing, unemployed Mexican American and Latinx actors and actresses ranging all across Hollywood, New York City, and beyond.[4]

Fede: A simulacra of ethnoracialized *and* gendered subjects, no? J-Lo is a case in point. As she's moved from TV to film to music video to TV she's swung like a pendulum from Latina (bad) to Anglo (good). As a fly girl in *In Living Color* (1990–14) she's all body—and all *bad*; as Marisa Ava Marie Ventura in the film *Maid in Manhattan* (2002), she's redeemed and good (after being bad for supposedly stealing a fur coat) in her association with aristocratic white-ness (Ralph Fiennes playing the character Christopher Marshall); in the music video "I Luh Ya Papí" (2014) she's all Latina derrière (bad); and in the 2016 TV series *Shades of Blue* (2016–18) she's the corrupted single *mamá,* Harlee Santos (bad once again).

In *Desperate Housewives* we also see this pendulum swing, and mostly toward the bad.

Gaby Solis (Eva Longoria) from "Any Moment," *Desperate Housewives*

Maria
The Housemaid

Gaby Solis (Eva Longoria) passes as the "good" citizen (upper middle-class white-picket-fence suburbanite) in a place like Wisteria Lane, only to swiftly swing to the "bad" citizen status *and* marked as Brown Other when her socioeconomic status shakes a little. When Carlos Solis (Ricardo Antonio Chavira) loses his job (blinded) and becomes a massage therapist, Gaby's no longer privy to the Wisteria Lane Country Club's front entrance and must use the servant's entrance at the back of the club.

Bill: Your riff on Eva Longoria from *Desperate Housewives* sent my mind racing back to her *Devious Maids* production gig. Have I told you about my new friend, "Maria"?[5] I don't know why it should surprise me that established tropes and stereotypes from the world of print media, film, and television should make the grand leap into the digital realm, but still they do. Take a minute and check out the "cool" animated special effects available to you at Motion VFX!

Who are they? MotionVFX is a registered trademark of a company called MotionVFX, which is created and owned by Szymon Masiak. Szymon is very well known in the computer graphic industry and has been working in it for over twenty years in areas like computer games, commercials, and major motion pictures.

Here are the rest of the digital animatronic beasts—Maria, who may be Afromex, stands out apart from Kevin, who's just a "kid," and Matt, just a "guy."

| Ann | Betty | Jenny | John | Kevin |
| The Businesswoman | The Grandma | The Doctor | The Businessman | The Kid |

| Maria | Matt | Rob | Sam | Will |
| The Housemaid | The Guy | The Builder | The Cool Girl | The Policeman |

But getting back to what you and I were just talking about, yes, of course, but we also have to complicate (not "problematize"—I am trying to wean myself off eighties-era jargon) these migrations between good and bad, Latinx and Anglo, right? Intercept the network logic of things. That's why I love the era of TV when I was coming of age—with shows like *CHiPs* (1977–83). When it comes to bad/good, Latinx/Anglo—all bets are off and all logic goes out the window.

Okay, stay with me, because this one is gnarly—Erik Estrada is one of the huge Latinx stars of twentieth-century American entertainment. For the record, Estrada was born in East Harlem, Manhattan, New York City; is the child of Carmen Moreno, a seamstress, and Renildo Estrada; and "is of Puerto Rican descent."[6]

But on TV in the seventies and eighties, Estrada played "Ponch," Officer Francis Llewellyn "Ponch" Poncherello, a California Highway patrolman. So he's in California, right, so he has to be Mexican American, as he is a Puerto Rican actor playing a Latino on network TV. But is he!? "Francis Llewellyn[!]

'Ponch' Poncherello" is a name that vaguely *sounds* Italian or Italian American, . . . sort of— no doubt the producers were trying to merely cash in on the homonymics of "Arthur Herbert Fonzarelli," aka The Fonz or Fonzie from ABC's *Happy Days* (1974–84) megashow.

In any event, the only reason viewers of *CHiPs* would ever hesitate to assign him to the proper eugenics silo, the sound of his last name, doesn't come into play, as Ponch is a womanizer/rake, aka a male Latino TV subject effect. This gloss from the IMDB website by a fan is so egregious and so on point, I have to quote it at length, as it saves me the time of glossing my arguments in *Tex[t]-Mex*:

CHiPs: Biography for Officer Frank "Ponch" Poncherello (Character) from "CHiPs" (1977)[7]

A hot-blooded Latino, joins the California Highway Patrol (CHiPs, motorized state police) totally undisciplined and unexperienced, [*sic*] looking like a hopeless case; fortunately his veteran partner Jon proves a good, loyal and patient teacher while Ponch pays his dues over and over, as his Latin temper doesn't exactly help, but slowly learns and given his brideless dedication in time makes their team the best in the force, even Sergeant Getraer, who always was on his case comes to trust and rely upon him too, enough to let them train new rookies. One thing comes naturally to the sexy hunk: he's a born charmer and enthusiastic womanizer, never abusive. (Author: V-kissers[8])

As I said, "priceless"—basically, "V-kissers" in his snarky gloss of the show manages to work in every Latina/o stereotype under the sun for Ponch—this bizarre "Italian" Latino trope/highwayman. But with THIS huge difference from other cinematic and televisual Latinxs—he's a good guy, a good cop, though he is known, the swarthy bastard, to cut corners here and there.

Allow me a quick flash forward to March 2017, when Hollywood issued a requisite rev/rehash of the TV show *CHiPs* called *CHIPS*, and starring, as Ponch, the talented Chicano actor Michael Peña.

Michael Peña as Frank "Ponch" Poncherello, *CHiPS* (2017)

I interrupt my own CHiPsian reverie to sample an interview that Peña and his director, Dax Shepard, had when the movie came out:

SHEPARD: Well "CHiPs" is the nickname that California Highway Patrol have. "CHiPs" or "Chippies." And it was a popular show from '77 to '83. And when I was a kid . . . Both of us [Peña is from Illinois] actually are from the Midwest, and it was grey and cold eight months of the year. And you would turn this show on and for an hour, you were in California with palm trees and beaches . . .

PEÑA: Bikinis.

SHEPARD: Bikinis. And this odd couple on motorcycles—this tall, lanky white dude and a Latino. So it was a cool original pairing that was appealing.

PEÑA: Yeah, I remember as a kid, you're like, "Where is that, mom?" You're looking at the screen like it's some island.

SHEPARD: "What world is that?"

PEÑA: Yeah, "What world is that?"

SHEPARD: "Where a Latino is the star. And the good guy!"[9]

Fede: Don't get me started on Shephard's filmic rehash of the TV show, Bill. And here we can't throw blame on anyone but Shephard; he also wrote the screenplay. Peña's Ponch is in *heat.* He's a sexual addict; he can't go but a few minutes before he either has to masturbate in the nearest restroom or hump the nearest *chica.* And, this without any sense of an ironic wink from Shephard's script or lens.

Bill: Of course! It's old hat as old hat! The Mexican as synecdoche (or shorthand) for a particularly dark, subterranean (usually heteronormative) brand of sexuality—I swear it's as old a trope as the whore with the heart of gold!

Fede: While not straddling a saddle-bagged Kawasaki chopper à la *CHiPs,* I'd say that Stephanie Beatriz (she plays Gloria's little sister, Sonia, in *Modern Family*) as Detective Rosa Diaz and Melissa Fumero as Detective Amy Santiago in the Golden Globe awardee, *Brooklyn Nine-Nine* (2013–), brings *CHiPS* into the twenty-first century.

Not only are they the badasses of the precinct; they are wicked smart and complex. (Notably, Stephanie Beatriz expressed interest in playing Marvel's lesbian Latina superhero, America Chavez.) This is the kind of #browntv that Isabel Molina-Guzmán identifies as "color-conscious" TV programing that "develop[s] characters with ethnic and racial cultural and experiential specificity and thereby more complexity."[10]

Stephanie Beatriz and Melissa Fumero clowning around
on the set of *Brooklyn Nine-Nine* (2013–)

Bill: Your reminder brings to mind a moment in an interview with Gloria Anzaldúa that I stumbled across last week while preparing my opening comments for the visit of Chicana *chingona* Myriam Gurba to our campus. Anzaldúa says:

> We need to concentrate not so much on victimhood, but on how we are liberating ourselves, how we are emancipating ourselves, and how we are empowering ourselves as Chicanas, as women. By rewriting, not just the myths, and by reinterpreting the goddesses we are creating a new culture.[11]

In a sense, Beatriz and Fumero allow us to overwrite (we can never erase) the strutting, motorcycle- (phallus-) hugging ridiculousness of Erik Estrada and Michael Peña. Beatriz and Fumero as reinterpreted Latinx goddesses for a twenty-first-century audience hungry for metamorphosis—of themselves *and* their tropes.

Fede: Color-conscious writing and casting of Latinx characters also happens in *Scrubs* (2001–10). Judy Reyes plays Carla Espinosa—a smart Latina who throws back in the face of the other cast of characters and the TV viewers a deep awareness and critique of all the stereotypes of Latinas. And this includes her African American love interest, Turk, who pigeonholes her as Mexican or Puerto Rican, and not the Dominican Latina that she is. Molina-Guzmán writes, "Reyes and the writers craft a character that exploits the documented tensions between experienced nurses, newly minted medical interns, and resident doctors for laughter instead of making the Latina character's ethnicity, gender, and sexuality the butt of the joke."[12] Carla, Rosa Diaz, and Amy Santiago as smart, strong Latina nurses and cops are stand-outs.

Mostly, however, with women and with men, #browntv replicates the kind of slip into stereotypes seen on the staid and stale TNT *Claws* (2017–). Here Judy Reyes plays Quiet Ann, the taciturn Latina lesbian who sports Ben Sherman or *pachuca*-styled sartorial wear in a show that otherwise thinks feminism is writing women as violent underworld kingpins.

#browntv is a complex animal, Bill.

Bill: I'd go so far as to declare that while high theorists like Roland Barthes, Jacques Derrida, and even Northrop Frye (Marshall McLuhan, in there as well) spun exegetic ruminations that were changing the terrain of interpretations, hermaphrodizing hermeneutics also, #browntv was throwing in complications of its own.

It had to. It has to.

Recently I have returned to the pages of James Baldwin to seek solace during our reign of neo-Fascist race hate—in particular against Latinx bodies, Mexican and Mexican American minds. In "Notes of a Native Son," Baldwin's singular essay, the African American sage seer of the twentieth century observes how the Black subject was "never looked at, but was simply at the mercy of the reflexes the color of one's skin caused in other people."[13] Of course, the Latinx subject provokes/triggers reflexes in at least two ways: true, the color of the skin, the physiognomy of the indigene emerges as a provocation; but also, then, there is the sound of our voices, the traces of a mother tongue that itself triggers rage (the sound shape of Spanish, the accent, the "mis" pronunciations). But you can't teach that away, or wish it away—haters, in Baldwin's words, are not "interested in facts," preferring instead their own toxic confabulations, "because this invention expresse[s] and corroborate[s] their hates and fears so perfectly."[14]

Fede: So, can we say that a dramedy like *Orange Is the New Black* (2013–) is hermaphrodizing #browntv? As the series progressed through its seasons (the seventh season debuting in 2019), the narrative moves the voice and agency from the Anglo Piper Chapman (Taylor Schilling) to the Latinas. I'm thinking not only of Dayanara Diaz (Dascha Polanco), who leads the prison revolution (season 5, episode 1), but also of the bilingual, hyperliterate, witty best friends: Maritza Ramos (played by Diane Guerrero) and Marisol "Flaca" Gonzales (played by Jackie Cruz).

Diane Guerrero, Dascha Polanco, and Jackie Cruz in a scene
from Season 4 of *Orange Is the New Black*

They're our modern-day *pícaras* or tricksters who operate just askew of the center to reveal deep truths about the sociopolitical underbelly of the prison system and global capitalism generally. And yet in the end I can't help but think that this kind of complexity and critique *can* only exist within the prison narrativescape. It's too much a threat. It must be contained.

Bill: Yes, I am with you on that one, Fede, but for now, I want to turn the clocks back once again to *CHiPs*. But the old-school *CHiPs*, OG *CHiPs*. On October 7, 1978, the "Disaster Squad" episode (season 2, episode 4) of TV's *CHiPs* airs on NBC—I am a seventeen-year-old high school junior, dreaming of Catholic school girls with their uniforms (a wicked anticipatory form of cosplay in my addled *frontera* mind) and dodging the menacing glances of panopticonic nuns (their eyes, ubiquitous; their glances omniscient—think HAL in Kubrick's *2001*) at St. Augustine High School in Laredo, Texas.[15] Director Gordon Hessler and writer Max Hodge serve up a veritable deconstruction of tropes focused on good and evil, Latinxs and Anglos—as well as an exposé on how little children have their worldviews smashed by news on TV (one can only imagine what we will have to deal with shortly with all the kids deranged by Donald Trump–laced headlines). Fans have documented the vague outlines of the show in succinct fashion, sharing how the episode keys in on how a "television news crew creates negative publicity for Jon and Ponch when they air edited news segments making the officers look bad."[16] IMDB's unattributed squib is even more succinct: "Ponch befriends a runaway four-year-old motorcycle enthusiast while Jon romances his divorcée mother. A sensationalist news crew dubbed the Disaster Squad pesters Ponch and Jon."[17]

What these glosses miss, however, is that "Disaster Squad" is a prescient if squalid (we are talking seventies/eighties TV drama!) TV anticipation of Dan Gilroy's disturbing *Nightcrawler* from 2014 (and featuring Jake Gyllenhaal in his creepiest role ever) and Sofia Coppola's 2013 *The Bling Ring*. This is not to mention classics like Steven Soderbergh's *Sex, Lies, and Videotape* from 1989, where the work of the camera determines reality for all concerned—Wilder's *Sunset Boulevard* (1950) and Powell's *Peeping Tom* (1960) the great grandfathers of the genre.

In "Disaster Squad," Ponch and Jon are shadowed by an abusive, intrusive TV crew from LA's "Channel 3." This marauding, camera-toting micro mob of paparazzi scour the highways for stories they can force-feed to the evening news. In the episode, Ponch (with Estrada showing all the acting range of a cardboard cut-out) holds back idled looky-loos on the interstate, while Jon saves a disgruntled worker about to kill himself.

Footage of all this later appears on Channel 3 as Ponch, Latino ne'er-do-well, pushes the TV crew around (breaking the heart of the "four-year-old motorcycle enthusiast" whose mom Officer Jon, Ponch's partner, is trying to woo!).

Without wasting too much more space on this seventies epic, the episode ends happily with Channel 3's camera crew turning against their smarmy crooked anchorman—the tables are totally turned as, at the end, and again evoking a scene that only a Borges, Baudrillard, and McLuhan ménage à trois could have imagined, Jon becomes cameraman, capturing a forced confession from the Channel 3 anchor by his camera crew, lensed by Jon, with Ponch looking on like some latter-day Fellini.

The moral of the story? The "Mexican" CHiPs officer is redeemed, Jon probably gets sued by a local television union, fake-news journalists are outed as corrupt, and our attempt to ferret out a consistent line of argument for #browntv is derailed again!

Fede: You're obsessed with Estrada, Bill.

Bill: Unabashedly so, and it has got to the point where he invades my art—I recently dreamed up this graphic to add to my portfolio of digitally warped #mextasy posters:
I love collage as an art praxis and am even fonder of vintage ads from the

"Erik Estrada, Lady Magnet" © Guillermo Nericcio García (2013)

1940s and 1950s. In my art, I like to juxtapose yesterday with the more recent past, always in an effort to foreground spectators, spectators that are always implicit, invisible, or absent in graphic representations of ethnic American bodies. You can see me toying with this above, with Estrada the object of affection for gaggles of adoring white housewives—Stepford "dames" besotted with the brown *vato*'s hot, Latino *charmingness*.

Fede: Until we're truly postrace, we'll necessarily slip into Manichean formulations, Bill. But I take your point and have myself argued this in many other venues: no matter the diametric stereotype, we as Latinxs are not passive, absorptive sponges. Yours and Peña's retrospective Poncherello reverie is a case in point. In the late seventies, as now, we actively metabolize more than passively consume. We distill and reconstruct in our imaginations and our narrative realizations, including today's BrownWebTV. I'm not only thinking about your own foray with MextasyTV, but also those nine-minute or so episodes of *East WillyB* (2011–) on YouTube have to be some of the best narrative reconstructions done yet of all that Manichean flotsam out there. More importantly, it turns the reconstructive gaze inward—to all the garbage we eject within our Latinx communities. This is #browntv at its best.

Bill: What really gets me is that we are living and breathing and writing now in the Golden Age of Television—forget Murrow or Cronkite; it's Matt Weiner with *The Sopranos* and *Mad Men* and Vince Gilligan with *Breaking Bad* (and now *Better Call Saul*) that represent the acme, the apex, the high summit of narrative power and ubiquity. And here again, the "Mexicans" we meet are scary, and horrible, and ridiculous as all get out. And what I call the "East Coast Latinx Gravity" is in full force here. By which I mean a kind of East Coast Latinx dominance—owing to the Puerto Rican density of New York City and the Cuban American hegemony in Miami, Florida. Two of the star villains on *Breaking Bad* (2008–13) and, now, *Better Call Saul* (2015–), are retreads from Brian De Palma's 1983 *Scarface* (a film we should talk about at some point as we chronicle the reverberations of #browntv): Steven Bauer, who played Manny Ribera to Italian American Al Pacino's "Cuban" Tony Montana, is "Don Eladio," a major cartel boss on Vince Gilligan's *Breaking Bad* prequel. Bauer, né Esteban Ernesto Echevarría Samson, in Havana, Cuba, is at least a Cuban–Cuban American, albeit playing a Colombian.

The second guy, who is a method actor with serious training chops, is Mark Margolis, who played Alberto the Shadow in *Scarface* and takes the role of the nefarious Hector Salamanca in *Breaking Bad* and *Better Call Saul.*

It's hilarious that Margolis plays the better "Mexican" than Bauer, whose version of Spanish makes my Spanish (and I am a recovering, English-dominant Pocho) seems like I trained at the *Real Academia Española.*

Margolis, a Jewish American actor from Philadelphia, studied at Temple University before hopping over to New York City, where he found himself under the tutelage of Stella Adler at the Actors Studio. His Mexican Spanish, while not epic, is believable, and you can hear the studied nuance of a professional East Coast trouper aping the cadences of Northern Mexican narcos. It's a *twofer*—we get yet another generation of Hollywood stars con-cretizing the notion of male Mexicans as crimi-nals, monsters, violent, vulgar, and dangerous; and the actors, in this case, are not even "Mexi-can," not even a trace of the motherland in their DNA (their passports, maybe, via vacations in Acapulco).

Viva Zapata, 1952. Anthony Quinn, as Pancho Villa, with (seated) Marlon Brando as Emiliano Zapata.

Fede: You're making me feel nostalgic for Anthony Quinn as Eufemio—even Brando in Brownface as his brother Emilio Zapata—in Elia Kazan's *Viva Zapata!* (1952).

Bill: At least I didn't bring up Charlton Heston as Mexico City narcotics detective Miguel "Mike" Vargas in *Touch of Evil*!

Fede: Welles was down—and a victim of the Hollywood "communist" purge—so I'm really not sure why he made the Brownface turn. You'd know the backstory better than me. What we do know well is that there's a long tradition of mainstream producers making safe the Brown Imaginary by casting nonthreatening Anglos or other non-Mexican Latinxs *as* Mex-heritaged characters. But, as you like to sleuth out in your work, there's always the slippery Latinx that gets away from them and that upturns all their identity-straightjacket nonsense. I'm thinking of Giancarlo Giuseppe Alessandro Esposito as Gustavo "Gus" Fring in *Breaking Bad* and *Better Call Saul.* Sure, biographically Esposito's Blitalian (Black and Italian), but when there are few (if any) Blatinxs in mainstream TV, perhaps his Africanicity troubles mainstream notions of what it means to be Latinx. His character's Blatinx from Chile by way of Mexico. And while he's still a gangster, he's arguably the smartest Blatinx on TV.

Bill: A complex character to be sure—and finally the complexity of the Global South worming its way through the national synapses—"Gus Fring, Black Latino": that, alone, will cause brows to frown from Poughkeepsie to the Dakotas. AND his Spanish is better than the aforementioned Steven Brauer's!

Fede: While on the topic of Brownface squared—casting of Puerto Ricans or Cubans as Mexicans, et cetera—let's not forget how Latinxs are cast (or not) as *voices* in animation.

Bill: True that, Fede. The "Man of a Thousand Voices" (including Speedy Gonzales!), Mel Blanc, was able to valorize and render immutable a certain *audio-existentia* of the lazy, laid-back, inebriated (possibly) "Mexican." And it was not just in his Warner Brother shorts; it was as a company player, part of the ensemble on the Jack Benny show, where his "Sy the Mexican" skits were utterly memorable.

But the drought of the Spanish language, with a decidedly "Mexican" overtone (Laredo, my hometown, was probably 97 percent Mexican / Mexican American in the 1960s and 1970s) coming out of my NBC/CBS delivered via rabbit ears made me laugh as a child in full delight—so novel was this recognized sound, this warm, long vowel cadence, that even Blanc's approximation of the thing was enough to get me smiling (this is one for your Cognitive Studies people, Fede, for sure!).

When I heard Blanc doing his thing, it was as if I existed in a way. I think this was what the first generation of *Movimiento*-era cultural critics (and I include Ariel Dorfman and Armand Mattelart in this, with their *Para Leer El Pato Donald*) got wrong and, in a way, had to get wrong when they were doing *their* thing; outing the anti-indigenous atrocities of mainstream "innocent" entertainment, they forgot or had to ignore one of the reasons it worked so well—that the talents involved were at the top of their game, the top of their craft: Carl Barks's Disney narratives represent a kind of sublime semiotic epiphany in the history of American comics, and Mel Blanc (like *SNL*'s Will Ferrell and, now, Kate McKinnon) was an uncanny parodic genius of the first order.

Fede: Mel Blanc as Speedy and years before as Pan Pancho on the radio show *Cisco Kid* (1942–48) carves into the history of mainstream-animation white voice actors in Brownface. Consider the orchestration of body movement in constructing a Latino as an antagonist with El Macho that's voiced by Al Pacino in *Despicable Me* (2010) and replaced by Benjamin Bratt for *Despicable Me 2* (2013) or Robin Williams's voice acting of Ramon in *Happy Feet 2* (2011).[18]

Bill: The tropes are so well established that these *gabachos/as* just have to slip on the pelts—a few months back, I did a guest visit for the San Gabriel Mission Playhouse for their Latin Wave retrospective that included a screening of Lupe

Velez in *The Gaucho* (1927), with her co-star Douglas Fairbanks (both are utterly amazing). Velez is sensational as the nameless "Mountain Girl," a sexually proactive and utterly bestial Latina vixen/spitfire/minx. Of course, sassy Velez transcends the trope she invents with her acting and body movements, but the die is cast, and the hot-blooded Latina is there for the ages!

Fede: There's a fine line between amazing and complicit, Bill. Let's not forget that we Latinxs have been complicit in the making of a Brownface—or Brownvoice—imaginary. Alongside Robin Williams's Ramon in *Happy Feet 2* there's the histrionic, sexed-up voice of Sofía Vergara as Carmen.

And, in *Oliver & Company* (1988), even my Latinx woke hero, Cheech Marín, hams up a heavily East-LA Spanish accent when playing the voice of the Chihuahua, Ignacio Alonzo Julio Federico de Tito (known simply as Tito).

If we scratch more surfaces we see how the doublings and triplings of Brownface go on ad infinitum. Cheech played Pan Pancho to Jimmy Smits's Cisco in the 1994 TV movie *Cisco and the Kid*. And, while *Cloudy with a Chance of Meatballs* (2009) gets it a little better, with Benjamin Bratt luxuriating in the code-switching identity of Manny, he's still embodying a character who is relegated to the body: he's a mostly taciturn, jack-of-all-trades mechanic. It's this same Latinx as all-body and whose use function is as a fixer or tool that informs Disney Junior's *Handy Manny* (2006–).

Ohio-born and raised director Lee Unkrich (co-director on *Finding Nemo*; *Monsters, Inc.*; and *Toy Story 2*) teamed up with co-director Adrian Molina (and with Lalo Alcaraz brought on as consultant) do more than just get it right with casting of Latinos like Benjamin Bratt, Edward James Olmos, Gael García Bernal, Cheech Marín, Herbert Siguenza, and many other Latinxs to voice all the Latinx characters in Disney's animated feature *Coco* (2017). It seems our white creatrixs (Ohioans and all) of our *reel* imaginary have finally *woke* to the importance of reaching out to their Latinx compadres for some cultural education. The result: we went out to see it in droves, and on both sides of the proverbial Tortilla Curtain. *Coco* was the highest-grossing film in Mexico's history.

Bill: The body—always the body. And, still, all too often, that Latino/a body links up with the pejorative, with being awful (if not *offal*). The ninth season of Larry David's *Curb Your Enthusiasm* features Lin-Manuel Miranda, of *Hamilton* fame, in a nuanced, calculated, brilliant role of Welles-style megalomaniac—that's the great part, but, as in episodes like "Never Wait for Seconds," which aired November 19, 2017, we also run into characters like the handyman Cesar, played with earnest Latino-ness by Dominican American (by way of Queens) Hemky Madera.

Anything else you need from me, you give me a call

In the episode, Cesar turns down a tip from Larry for ridding his office of a humming noise, but, in lieu of the money, does keep asking favors. The short of it (like every episode of *Curb,* the plotting is bewilderingly labyrinthine) is that Cesar and his family end up using Larry's friend's Marty Funkhouser's posh swimming pool—and Little Cesar, son of Cesar, leaves said pool "befouled."

Dirty California Mexicans, once again, by way of the Dominican Republic—we just can't help but shit in the pool, the brown emanations of our bodies somehow echoing the brown patina of our skin.

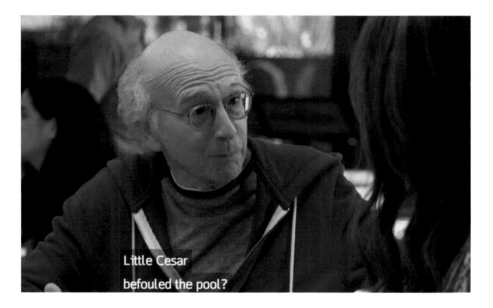

Little Cesar

befouled the pool?

One step forward, two steps back.

Back in 2007 I taught a graduate seminar in Literature/Cultural Studies called "Ethnic Mannequins or the Obscene Machine." Your writing of a relegation to the body got me thinking again in that vein, or to be honest, thinking for the first time really about the body as a relegation.[19] Weird—it is almost classically Catholic—truly! In the class, I was thinking about if we think of stereotypes as a species of puppet or mannequin, who then are their authors, their agents, their puppeteers? Extending this allegorical premise, who builds and finances the theater within which these puppets *play*? and why are we such a captive, supportive audience? We know (but forget as we lose a sense of self and walk into the narrative) that film and fiction hand us artifacts that traffic in verisimilitude. In that seminar, I ultimately concluded that we, enlightened critics though we were, were also at once agents in a (once analog and now digital) commerce of illicit fictional exchanges—players in an economy of the *ob-scene,* which grows even more complex when we attend to categories of ethnicity and gender. Here's a snapshot from the online gateway to that seminar (though I'm not sure that it assists us in our #browntv odyssey).

english 725 | spring 2007

ethnic mannequins or the obscene machine
a graduate seminar on film & literature via ethnic american theory and gender studies

A screengrab from the personal digital collection of Guillermo Nericcio García[20]

Fede: I'm glad you put a spotlight on the Latin prefix *ob* in *obscene,* Bill.[21] Indeed, some of those Latinx actors and actresses that appear at first glance to be manipulated by TV showrunner puppeteers are in fact simultaneously moving audiences "toward" and then "against" the scene. Let me return to a gesture made: J-Lo's "I Luh Ya Papí," shot by Dominican director Jessy Torrero (who interned on Darnell Martin's *I Like It Like That,* 1994).

I teach this regularly in my "Introduction to Latinx Pop Culture" course. At first, the students jump all over it, critiquing how J-Lo continues to be the object of the male, sexualized gaze—and this, even though she has beautiful, near-naked men draped all over her. They can't get over her bling and Daisy Dukes in the sudsy carwash scene. Then I return them to the opening framing device that sets up this instance of the *ob-scene.*

A white producer suggests different framing devices to J-Lo and pals, including shooting the music video at a waterpark, the carnival, and at the zoo. With this laundry list of ways that Latinxs have been stereotyped—

wet-T-shirt hypersexualized to animalistic—and with the script and camera clearly making fun of the white producer character, J-Lo with Torrero moves audiences against a long tradition of hypersexualized, all-corporeal, animalistic stereotypes of Latinxs. To make sure audiences get this, the (*ob*)*scene* ends with J-Lo and her pals asking, "Why do men always objectify the women in every single video? Why can't we for once objectify the men?" Then, we review the music video and suddenly are attuned to the fact that it's not just about "I luv ya *papí*" but also "I luv ya *mami*." They see how thoroughly she's in control of the puppet strings in this ob-scene gender-flip music video.

Bill: I love what you are able to do in the classroom for your students—it's a case of retraining the eye or, maybe, even, training the eye to see for the first time. All of it is pretty prehistoric—I mean Plato's *Republic* Book VII, with its legendary Allegory of the Cave (I believe only Laura Mulvey's "male gaze" essay gets more ink), laid out the myriad ways we are subjected, subject ourselves, are subject people to paralyzed and paralyzing stereotypical tropes. In my art, I have begun to try to play with these contradictions and hypocrisies, of others and my own. Take my piece *I/Eye Eva,* from my traveling "circus of *desmadres,*" Mextasy—a pop-up exhibition featuring Latina/o stereotypes and stereotype-exploding Latinx art:

At first glance, the "message" of the images is clear: Eva Longoria, Marionette. One of the most popular American stars in television in the late twentieth and early twenty-first century, Eva Longoria re-embodies the form and allure of the Latina bombshell, born in the early days of Hollywood. Like some reincarnation of Rita Hayworth, Raquel Welch (not dead yet, thank you very much), or Dolores del Rio, Longoria's sultry satin/Latin allure tempts the eyes of spectators and Nielsen ratings mavens from coast to coast.

I/Eye Eva picks up on the idea of the "ethnic mannequin" that I toyed around with in *Tex[t]-Mex* and in my aforementioned graduate seminar—there, in a mad synthesis of ideas lifted from Gayatri Spivak (the subject effect), Jacques Derrida (the trace), Frantz Fanon (darkness and psychopathology), and Edmundo Desnoes ("Cuba Made Me So" | Latina/o objectification), I tried to document the dynamic processes wherein Latina/o archetypes transmogrify/evolve.

What's special about Eva (and what she has in common with Rita Hayworth) is that she is the head of her own production companies and businesses—not all too successful if Wikipedia's resources are accurate (look up her defunct Beso restaurant biz based out of Vegas).

This connection between the star (the "victim" in the familiar objectification-of-woman argument) and the semiotic means of production surrounding her (graphic) reproduction complicates things for the contemporary arbiter of Latina semiotic signage. The piece above grafts together photography by Chilean camera wizard Nino Muñoz, in British lads' magazine *Arena*'s January 2007 issue, as well as work from the June 2009 issue of *GQ Mexico* (still looking for the photographer's identity). Two years apart, a twentieth-century ethnic mannequin stars in two photoshoots that feature images with ropes and chains, each image evoking unseen puppeteers of sorts. Coincidence? I would have to ask Eva and am still waiting on a callback![22]

One last thing about music videos and #browntv: one of the sharpest memories I have about Mexican Americans on television derives from a bit later in my development. I am talking about the Los Lobos album *Kiko*, produced by Mitch Froom at Sound Factory West Studio—it appeared on Slash Records, a Warner Brothers outlet, on May 26, 1992. I was a second-year assistant professor at SDSU when it came out, and of course, I was an audio slave to its fusion of rock and Mexican folk—#auralmextasy, as I tag it on my social media sites. Cesar Diaz's piece on *PopMatters* nails it:

> What makes *Kiko* exceptional is not just the ability to redefine a genre, but its inherent influence on a generation of artists. Bands like Ozomatli, Quetzal, and even Wilco owe a trick or two from *Kiko*. Ozomatli's career is dependent on Los Lobos right down to the Southern California band's offbeat lyricism to its rhythmic cumbias. Quetzal's Latin soul on 2003's *Worksongs* works the

same career blueprint of Los Lobos. Wilco's *Yankee Hotel Foxtrot* owes its sonic structure more to Los Lobos and producer Mitchell Froom than they do to Radiohead. It's easy to compare Wilco's direction on *Yankee Hotel Foxtrot* to the English band, and although it does merit some reference, it's obvious Wilco recognizes the impact of the East Los Angeles band. It was apparent at the inaugural Austin City Limits Festival in 2001, when Jeff Tweedy became a spectator during the Los Lobos' explosive set.[23]

Randall Roberts, in the *Los Angeles Times*, picks up the story:

To write their remarkable 1992 album *Kiko,* Hidalgo and Perez rented a space behind a bookstore on Whittier Boulevard. As told in "Dream in Blue," the team worked on what Morris describes as "highly impressionistic" songs. The band then worked out the material in a seedy place in L.A.'s skid row, and when it was time to record, brought in producer Mitchell Froom and engineer Tchad Blake. Recalled Perez of the process: "We were sticking mics down drainpipes and in the middle of a galvanized trash can. Mitchell would bring in an Optigan and all this crazy keyboard stuff, backwards guitars—all this stuff that we were really having fun with. But at the same time, something else was happening because we had cleaned the slate. We were wide open for things to come. We had cleaned out the cobwebs."[24]

But it is the award-winning video that ruptured my synapses, or, better put, subjected me to a kind of permanent metamorphosis.

Voted the Best Breakthrough Video at the MTV Awards in 1993, this surreal cinematic wonder was directed by Ondrej Rudavsky and edited by Bruce Ashley.

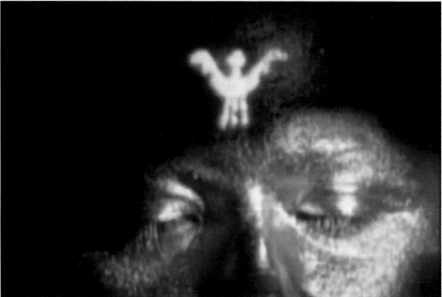

Chris Morris, writing in *Los Lobos: Dream in Blue,* calls Rudavsky's miniopus as a "traffic-stopping video"—concluding that Rudavsky's video is a "mind-bending, hallucinogenic melding of George Melies and Timothy

Leary."[25] Filled with ciphers, symbols, codes, and a dense sensual iconography worthy of Peter Greenaway, Rudavsky evokes the Latinx dreamscape implicit and explicit in Los Lobos's music and lyrics, creating a watershed progressive moment in the history of #brownTV.

Fede: Los Lobos, Latinx transmogrifications and lensing that breaks chains, Bill, I think we're ready to move from *pinche* paradoxes to our next section, *"Sombreros* to *Pistoleros." Adelante*!

Sombreros to Pistoleros

Fede: In the last section, we discussed the paradoxical ways in which Latinxs are constructed and reconstructed in the #browntv imaginary. In a way, we're externalizing our collective anxiety around this sense of at once being present, but then absent in our presence as well as being absent, but then present in our absence. I propose that in this section we dig deeper into the *bad* part of the equation in all its discomforting—and *threatening*—permutations: from no-good layabouts to bang-'em-up *pistoleros* and gangbangers.

As such, let's begin at, well, the pre-TV beginning: the repellent twelve-reel behemoth, D. W. Griffith's 1915 *Birth of a Nation.* As D. W. Griffith's camera pans left to right, and before it settles on its images that glorify the Aryan nation, Mexicans are mostly portrayed as layabouts.

Griffith's skill as a director is undeniable. He was able to take his enormous camera equipment places not seen before. He has an extraordinary eye for framing up artful mise-en-scènes. Yet, in the end, the experience of *Birth of a*

Nation, and of course all other films, is a gestalt whereby we take in both form *and* content. In this case, the no-holds-barred racism tears across those positive emotions generated by the aesthetic.

Bill: And we emerge from the dark transformed—in the dark, we are first transfixed by the uncanny "magic" of motion pictures paralyzing the psyche in remarkable ways so that the seductive administration of light and sound penetrates us to the core. But from this state of transfixion (trans-*fiction,* also?), we quickly move to a metamorphosis or transmogrification whereby Griffith's visionary epic displaces (infects?) whatever learned material was in our mind in the first place—and in this case, one suspects that Griffith's opus fell onto an audience whose mind's eye was filled with one part caricatures and one part tabula rasa.

Birth of a Nation, then, is the birth of cinema, and the simultaneous instantiation of a particular and peculiar way of thinking about the history of race (and history itself) from then to now.

Fede: Some two hundred million people have seen *Birth of a Nation,* emerging from Griffith transmogrified both for bad and for good. Dare I say: Griffith's camera obscura created our modern racialized consciousness—our modern-day #browntv.

Bill: It is true and not an exaggeration. In *Tex[t]-Mex* I argued that *Touch of Evil* was a key film, not just owing to the fact that it served as a last-chance comeback for the legendary Orson Welles—it was also key to the history of film and TV studies, as *Touch of Evil* was the movie that ace film-studies guru Stephen Heath used to basically found the field of critical film theory for *Screen.* Hence, every one of his premises (that break down) over the body/bodies of "Mexicans" and Mexicans in *Touch of Evil* can be seen to be imported into all the body of studies that coalesce under the moniker of film studies to the present. Imagine, then, the impact of Griffith—whose lensed narratives trace the semiotic DNA of cinema from *Birth of a Nation* to *Machete.*

Fede: It's worth reminding our readers that the early silver screen *was* the TV of the early twentieth century. It serialized episodic adventures, many of which were in Brownface. I'm thinking of Douglas Fairbanks donning his black mask in the silent *Mark of Zorro* (1920).

While upper-crust nineteenth-century *Californio hacendados* luxuriate in dandy rituals, the Latinx commoners are portrayed as brown untouchables. Only hiding behind a mask and in the cover of night does Zorro dare to slum it

In California, nearly a hundred years ago, with its warmth, its romance, its peaceful beauties, this dread disease, oppression, had crept in.

Then—out of the mystery of the unknown——appeared a masked rider who rode up and down the great highway —punishing and protecting— and leaving upon the vicious oppressor

with the brown *mestizo* Others. Masks allow for transgression—and transcendence—of the racialized Manichean imaginary.

Bill: Rescreening these old classics for this book, I am reminded just how little room there was in the past for the vagaries of nuance. As if there was no room for gray, certainly no room for any random Pantone fusion between black and white. In *Mark of Zorro* the good are *good*, and the bad are bad; the rich are rich, and the poor are oppressed—or whipped de Sade–style, as what happens with the priest above.

I said above that the die was cast and I mean that in the literal sense—one witnesses in screening these movies from yesterday the forging of casting elements (tropes, stereotypes, clichés) that will shape the entertainment industry into the present. The oppressed masses that Zorro saves are the great grandfathers of the mice living in trash or drunk and singing odes to marijuana that fill the mise-en-scène in Warner Brothers' Speedy Gonzales cartoons.

And the funny thing is that these mutations, these cinematic monstrosities don't stay within our borders—they flow without, contaminating and infecting the imaginations (and the semiotic imaginary) of folks south of the border. Look below here at this Mexican lobby card from 1959 for a re-release of 1937 Republic movie serials starring John Carroll and Helen Christian. The knife-wielding Latino swarthy thug confronting Zorro is classic.

Fede: And then of course we have *El Murcié-lago Negro*! *El Murciélago Negro,* also known to our English-speaking compatriots as *Batman,* wasn't so original when Bob Kane introduced this comic book superhero in 1939—Zorro *and* our Mexican masked luchadores had already paved the way. All three figures mixed and matched in my nascent brain as a kid in Mexico, then in Califas, cross-dressing and border-crossing as Zorro, Blue Demon, and the Bat. I'm going to claim this as an instance of pop Latinx decolonial resistance. Where the flesh-and-blood brown Mexican subject reinhabits tired white-savior icons. It's what would have happened had Robert Rodriguez, instead of the Anglo Martin Campbell, been allowed to reboot *The Mask of Zorro* in 1998. Because of big fights with producers from Columbia Pictures, Rodriguez stepped away from its making. Campbell served up more of the Brownface same: Hopkins as the wizened Zorro, Antoñio Banderas as Alejandro Murrieta (fictional brother of Joaquin Murrieta), and English-accented actress Catherine Zeta-Jones as the feisty Latina love interest, Elena Montero. We can only speculate as to what *Mask of Zorro* would have been had Robert Rodriguez been at the helm; his Latinx *rasquache,* guerilla-style approach scared the heebie-jeebies out of producers at Paramount.

Bill: Ha, and imagine if he had dragged Quentin Tarantino along for the reiteration of this long chain of Hollywood "magic"—it's funny: there is nothing magic at all about this repetition, this repetition compulsion. Zeta-Jones as hot-blooded Latina, why not!? "It's all good box office."

Fede: Of course, Batman/Zorro are part of a much larger white/*criollo*-savior to hapless Latino, manifest-destiny mythos. The genre that seemed to deepen and spread wide this mythos has to be the Western. The great *pensador* Wittgenstein loved his Westerns. The clear-cut good-versus-evil Manichean formula put his brain to rest. But within this good versus evil there's this perpetuation of a racialized and racist imaginary.

Bill: True that, Fede. Consider these panels by Curt Swan and Murphy Anderson from 1972:

Growing up in Laredo, Texas, ensconced in my room with Snoopy posters and UT Longhorn banners (picture Rusty Brown from Chris Ware's short stories, but not so weird!), I always thrilled to the wonders of Curt Swan and Murphy Anderson's *Superman* stories for DC Comics. Little did I know that one of these wonders—January 1972, issue 247—featured the Man of Steel as a defender of Mexican farmworkers. Small world. A former student of mine and regular contributor to my online blog, Dr. Marc García-Martinez, of Hancock College, wrote to me back in the day about this particular and peculiar blast-from-the-past comic book:

At the end of the tumultuous 60's decade *Time Magazine* featured Cesar Chavez on its famous cover and a timely story on "The Grapes of Wrath, 1969: Mexican-Americans on the March." At the beginning of 1980 *National Geographic*, that distinguished magazine devoted to all things natural and cultural, featured an honest piece on "Mexican-Americans: A People on the Move." Somewhere in between, circa 1972, DC comics contributed its own unique brand of homage to *La Raza* by presenting a peculiar tale in its Superman No. 247 that could have justly been called "Mexican-Americans: Idle Farm Workers on Attack." Features in the climax of the story are an assortment of Mexican (*ergo* geographically-laborious-American) farm workers in California's central valley. The tale is an ironic and curious little portrait of the Mexican, that seems to cut too close to the spineless, indolent, leech-off-the-government for aid portrayals we've seen all too often lately. This is some strange verbal-visual *caca* here, *carnal* . . . perhaps inadvertent. Let's chat about this some more![1]

The great white savior from America, come to Mexicans (the domestic US-based flavor *and* exotics to the south of the Rio Grande) to save the day. To this very moment this continues; I just recently screened *Batman v Superman: Dawn of Justice* (2016), directed with utter ineptness by the unfortunate Zack Snyder—pardon the snark, as it is clear from the release cut that many, many executive producers and bean-counters got their paws on the film as it was making its way to release. The scene where Henry Cavill as the Man of Steel saves the day in Mexico is epic—there is no irony in the image (what I mean to say is that there are barrels of irony, but none evident to the filmmakers). The adoring Mexicans, some even in *Día de los Muertos* facepaint (yikes), cling to Superman with a passionate sycophantish longing, as if the very touch of his

white(?) super substance will imbue them with a reason to live. The semiotics are priceless.

Fede: Don't get me started, Bill. Zack Snyder's Christological shitsmear all over his Superman flicks gags us with messianic crucifixions and resurrections, all the while either recreating us as mystical and hapless—or erasing us altogether. Snyder's Metropolis has no Latinxs, unless you count Soledad O'Brien's cameo as a news reporter. In Snyder's earlier *Man of Steel* (2013), I counted two Latinxs: the gas station attendant and a Latina infantry soldier who tries to take the red-caped messiah down. Clearly, from Snyder's distillation and reconstruction of the building blocks of reality where we are the majority minority, he deliberately chooses to erase us. And when he finally does put us in front of the camera, it's worse than Swan and Anderson's 1972 *Superman* that you mention above.

Recall that just prior to this scene that you mention, Superman has just saved Metropolis from high-tech invading Kryptononians. Then Snyder has him fly south of the border to Juarez to rescue a girl from a burning building—a burning building, and not a high-tech alien invasion. What I'm getting at is how Snyder uses the silver screen to depict us as helpless; we can't even save a child from a burning building. And, when our Zorro avatar shows up, aka Batman, the script has him tangentially reference his Native American ancestry: it's in his *nature* to be a hunter. For the record, Snyder's not the only supremacist. David Goyer and Chris Nolan are given writing credits.

Don't get me wrong. I think Chris Nolan's Batman trilogy is hands down the best superhero film fodder going. But remember, and this is a big bone I pick in *Latinx Superheroes in Mainstream Comics,* it's Nolan who decided to cast the Brit Tom Hardy as Bane—the most intelligent, complex supervillains in the DC universe who *is* Latino. This shamefully deliberate erasure was a seriously missed opportunity to set the record straight. We could've had Jimmy Smits, Michael Peña, Benjamin Bratt, Wilson Cruz, or any number of other Latinos cast as Bane. Instead, we get the same old, same old.

Bill: Oh, for the wonderful times of the 1960s, when Cubano/Spaniard Cesar Romero was eating up the screen, white makeup covering up his swarthy Latinesque mustache as Batman's nemesis, the Joker.

Romero's antics as the Joker, later played by Jack Nicholson and the late Heath Ledger on the big screen, set the stage for an interpretation of the Joker that was outsized and really funny (and evil)—not that Romero's performance was going to win an Emmy, but his onscreen antics somehow surpassed the

aesthetics of a show that has gone down in history for its kitschy, campy narrative protocols.

Or, better, come with me back to the 1970s—when Phoenix, Arizona–born wonder Lynda Carter romped all over my TV set as *Wonder Woman.* Here you have an Amazon portrayed by a Chicana kicking ass in ridiculous plots that make Adam West's Batman look like high drama. Yet every now and then there were episodes like "The Fine Art of Crime," directed by Dick Moder and written by Anne Collins (season 3, episode 4, October 13, 1978).

The episode finds Wonder Woman investigating "a series of robberies that lead her to a faux artist (Roddy McDowall[!]) who uses a device to turn people into living statues to help him commit his crimes. Wonder Woman falls into a trap, is turned into a statue and is exhibited at a museum."[2]

Here viewers are confronted not with a whitewash of racialized hierarchies as we were with *Superman v Batman,* nor the mind-numbing paternalism of Superman in his DC Comics / Mexico adventure. What we have here is a kitschy TV program theatricalizing the absurdity of its own costuming, role-playing, et cetera, but, at the same time, and at the level of the televisual subterranean, valorizing a female hero who just happens to be Latina.

Legions of fans from East LA to San Antonio joined Lynda Carter fan clubs hoping to emulate her success as actress, but also the clever, beautiful superhero whose costume she filled.

The symbolism is clear—though Wonder Woman is ostensibly a visitor from her Amazonian origins, she is also, at once, an avatar of the US via the

United Nations—a Nazi-fighting heroine whose fusion of superpowers, gender, and, yes (once again), sexy, nationalism-infected costume makes for an overdetermined irresistibility. And yet, Carter is not only beautiful; her sexualization does not mask her equally dreamy role on the show as an intellectual and government attaché—an agent of the Inter-Agency Defense Command. But we don't have to be aficionados of Baudrillard or Freud to note that while playing a role she is also, at once, a Latinx avatar/actress from Phoenix, Arizona—and, in a sense, something sadly missing from the terrain of entertainment in the present moment.

Fede: My *Mexipina niña,* Corina, adores Wonder Woman. Back when she was barely out of diapers, she shunned the princess outfits and instead went for Wonder Woman costumes—and all because of Lynda Carter. As I mentioned at the beginning of this book, I don't have cable TV. Yet, there's the trusty internet to introduce new generations to our generation's #browntv fodder. Ironically, I had to turn the clock back to 1978 for Corina to finally get her Latina superhero. Corina's a Tweenx now. She doesn't dress up as Wonder Woman, but she's becoming an excellent critical consumer of pop culture: she collects all variety of Wonder Woman (Gal Gadot) action figures that she then reframes (often dismembered) within her various collage art works.

It's as if seventies-TV *Wonder Woman*'s "Fine Art of Crime" episode predicted this moment, but with a *Mexipina* twist. As you point out, the dastardly Henry Roberts (Roddy McDowall) and partner in crime, Moreaux (Michael McGuire), think they've turned Wonder Woman into a *fine art* statue, but their high-tech wizardry's not enough to turn this Latina to stone. She can't be reified. Unlike a Lichtenstein, Latinx pop culture resists high-art reframing. Corina doesn't just sit her Wonder Woman figures on a shelf somewhere. Her *Mexipina* imagination animates and breathes life into something that otherwise has a fixed functionality. The next step: to have our new-gen Latinxs bump the Zach Snyders off the log to breathe ethnoracial life into these superheroic icons.

There's an important detail I don't want us to overlook, Bill. The lasso. Our Latina Wonder Woman's golden Lasso of Truth that forces supervillains (mostly male) to obey her and tell the truth. In *The Secret History of Wonder Woman,* Jill Lepore connects the dots between Wonder Woman's creator, William Moulton Marston, and his living with both his wife and his mistress and the suffrage movement. In and through the creation of a superhero from the Amazon—our modern-day Latina—all sorts of shackles were being shed in and around sexuality and gender roles chez Marston. Keep in mind that for all of Marston's feminist enlightenment, he hadn't yet clued into issues of race. Marston's *Wonder Woman* #19 (1946) is a case in point. He has Africans speaking "gibu doggo" and sporting swastikas.

Bill: Lepore's chronicle is something else; Marston's wife Elizabeth Holloway, with mistress Olive Byrne, filled Marston's life and imagination with female powerhouses and targets for his kinks—it's good to know that genre fiction, associated with the banal and the conventional, flows from such fertile subterranean yearnings.

And then there's the Western, right? Cowboys and *their* lassos!

Fede: The lasso is the vaquero's main tool; cowboys use it to direct cattle—to get them to obey. It's become an important symbol and stand-in for the Anglo frontiersman's manifest destiny, something that beats at the heart of other foundational Brown televisual imaginings: *Bonanza* (1959–73).

Bill: Oh yes, *Bonanza* and *The High Chaparral*—two high points in my gallery of influential screen memories (along with *Land of the Lost*, which sadly we won't have room for here in this collection—Chaka as Chicano?). But before we get to those TV Westerns, a sidebar. By the time cowboys, and bandits (so many Mexican bandits that it appears to be our vocation, our calling), made their way to the boob tube, pulp fiction magazines and cinema had laid the groundwork for the naturalization of the "Mexican" as pejorative—Academic historians, too, had done their yeoman's work *pejoratizing* the Latino, as Américo Paredes's underestimated masterwork *With His Pistol in His Hand: A Border Ballad* shows with *ganas* and conviction.[3]

Some key examples, seen below, will suffice, cribbed from the online pages of my *Tex{t}-Mex Galleryblog,* now enjoying its thirteenth year online:

The curator at the Comic Book Stories is a tireless servant to our compulsive appetite for garish stereotypes. The latest entry with tawdry *Spicy Western Stories* samples has almost every flavor of ethnic sexuality/criminality and

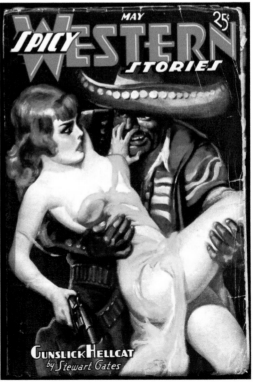

swarthy viciousness that one might imagine. The year 1937 was particularly good for scary "Mexican" covers with two, by H. J. Ward, that belong in the *Tex[t]-Mex* Stereotypes Hall of Fame.

These garish posters are priceless—they go a long way to informing how it is that stereotypes become enmeshed in the masses' subterranean psyche; Jameson, back in the day, schooled us in the Political Unconscious—but this is something more visceral and sensual. And all this graphic excess is persuasive, informing and shaping Hollywood's continued efforts since Griffith to render the ethnic body as naturally (naturalized? naturalizing?) prone to acts of sexual/criminal violence—think here of Alfonso Bedoya as "Gold Hat" (as with Lupe Velez, aka "Mountain Girl," in *The Gaucho,* the Brown subject *has no name*) playing opposite Humphrey Bogart in John Huston's *The Treasure of the Sierra Madre* (1948). Bedoya / Gold Hat's "I don't have to show you no stinking badges" epithet representing a kind of apex of sorts (till we get to Roberto Rodriguez's and Danny Trejo's deconstructive re-rendering of the same in *Machete*).

What is weird is just how widespread the Mexican bandit trope was—I recently stumbled upon *Whirligig.* A website dedicated to the show places it in

The Treasure of the Sierra Madre lobby card from the private collection of Guillermo Nericcio García. Alfonso Bedoya, as Gold Hat, confronts Humphrey Bogart, aka Dobbs.

context as "one of the first exponents of variety on children's television . . . a fortnightly Saturday afternoon treat, which began in November 1950, devised by Michael Westmore and which was the very first children's programme to be broadcast live from the BBC studios in Lime Grove." "Mr. Turnip," who maintains pages on *TurnipNet,* is quite moving with his mishmash of maudlin nostalgia and badly web-designed nineties-era html, continues: "merely to mention *Whirligig* is to invite sighs of nostalgia." *Whirligig* alternated with other Saturday-afternoon children's programs then on television.

So what, right? Just some forerunner of *Captain Kangaroo,* which debuted in 1955, correct?

Not so fast, #browntv fans (and fans, also, of Native American scapegoating)! The show featured regular sequences with puppets and prehistoric animation with Pete, the cowboy, and, you guessed it, a Mexican bandit and a Native American Indian. Take it away, Mr. Turnip:

> Hank the Cowboy Rides Again
> 　　HOWDY FOLKS!!
> 　　Would you like your old pal Hank to tell you a story? You would? Well it was likey this. . . .
> 　　*So began Hank the Cowboy tales with his goofy horse (his 'old timer'), Silver King and Big Chief Dirty Face ("Me Big Chief Dirty Face, Me always in disgrace") along with Mexican Pete the Bandit who sang to the tune of The Mexican Hat Dance:*

The unassuming viewer, perhaps a child, perhaps a distracted adult, opens their eyes to a mid-1950s conjuring of stereotypes that are as awful as they are comprehensive!

> 　　"I'm Mexican Pete, zee bad bandit
> 　　Zee bad bandit I always 'ave bin
> 　　I tie Senor Hank to zee railroad
> 　　An' zat is zee end of 'im !"
> 　　"I'm Mexican Pete ze bad bandit
> 　　I've captured the little Cassy
> 　　Senor Hank he must pay ze fat ransom
> 　　Before little Cassy I free"

Mexican Pete, perpetrator of attempted murder, or Mexican Pete, kidnaper of helpless white damsels. The next stanza, odd as it is absurd, seems to suggest that our "Mexican" is not the heroic bandit his boasts make him out to be:

"I'm Mexican Pete ze bad bandit
Zees onions they makea me cry
Please letta me out of zis kitchen
Poor Mexican Pete he will die!"

Last, Mr. Turnip clues us in to the other feature players on the show, including "Hank's nephew, [the aforementioned] Cassy, Freddie Parrot and Little He-He (son of Big Chief Laughing Gas and Minnie Ha-Ha)." And, of course, we can't keep readers of #browntv from pictures of these pre-animatronic ethnic American monstrosities designed for the eager eyes (and impressionable psyches) of England's children. In the first figure here, Mexican Pete the Bandit, forces a tied-up child to witness his terrorist bombing:

In the next episode, we meet the cast of characters including Silver King, the horse, Hank the Cowboy, and, now in puppet form (a man by the name of Francis Coudrill was the puppeteer), Pete (the Bad Bandit)—it is not enough that the "Mexican" be identified as a "Bandit"; he must also immortalized as a "Bad" Bandit, lest viewers have the chance of being confused!

Who knew we would get to travel to Merry Ol' England in our textual autopsy of our #browntv!?

Fede: I'm glad you brought this up, Bill. Honestly, the farther I travel from our shores in any given direction the more racist the Latinx stereotype. Here we have not only a *bandido* but a terrorist who tortures a child. I know #browntv's been getting it so wrong for so long, but when you compare it with what's going on in the rest of the world—well, it's caricatures of caricatures squared, Bill.

With this in mind, and this may sound strange, I can look back with gooey-eyed nostalgia to a show like *Bonanza* that first hit Saturday-night TV sets (and in color) in 1959. This was about ten years before I was birthed into what would quickly become one of the world's most magnificent and monstrous of megalopolises, Mexico City. The show ran right into 1973, when I was still in diapers, but there were plenty of reruns that I'd catch at my *abuelita*'s when I was older. Looking back at some of those shows today, it seems positively progressive—social justice progressive at that.

Bonanza was all about writing narratives and characters that set right social wrongs. It messes with notions of white purity (all the brothers are half-brothers, with Little Joe's *mamá* a French Creole), and it transgresses racial taboos. In "The Fear Merchants" (season 1, episode 20), the writers give screen time to Hop Sing's uncle, who celebrates the affirmation of Chinese culture and ancestry. And, this episode includes a scene that clearly depicts the xenophobia of the town's Anglo cowboys; they beat Hop Sing senseless, with one of the rednecks declaring: "gonna have to clean a lot more of this dirt outta here before Virginia City's a place fit to live." The script, lensing, editing, and sound all seek to trigger empathy for Hop Sing in the televisual audience.

Bill: . . . and coming online after *Bonanza* but sharing the airways at the same time is *High Chaparral*, with its aforementioned Boriqua star Henry Darrow as Manolito—I love the way this adoring fan site glosses his character:

> Lover, activist, carouser, peacemaker—all describe the multi-faceted brother of Victoria Cannon, Manolito Montoya. [. . .] Manolito is looking for something, something that he cannot put into words, but something that he knows he'll recognize when he sees it. His restlessness of soul manifests itself in many ways, but most often in his pursuit of women. [. . .] This appetite for the ladies has made the rift between himself and Don Sebastian even wider, for his reputation is such that no respectable marriageable woman would ally herself with him. [. . .] He is also a compromiser, a peacemaker, and this is best demonstrated by his attitude and treatment toward the Apache people. He understands their desire to be free on their own land, and he respects them. He is a tireless translator between John and the neighboring tribes, and advocates their fair treatment at every turn. Manolito has a political side, too. If a cause seems worthy to support, he will lend his support, whether that cause is feasible or not. From Irish miners to his own oppressed people, Manolito's compassion

cannot allow him to remain silent when he sees injustice. His innate prudence may urge another tactic than direct conflict, but he doesn't leave an injustice un-addressed. Manolito has the makings of a potential political savior.[4]

Sounds like an avatar of exceptionalism for some future #browntv ideal, no?

Actor Darrow was christened Enrique Tomás Delgado when he bounced onto the planet, and it is telling that he was aware at the time exactly what his role, his presence, his face (if not his original name) meant for Americans of Latin American descent: "I am happy to have given Latin Americans a hero they can identify with."[5]

Fede: During this *Leave It to Beaver* TV squeaky-clean epoch (i.e., straight, Anglo master narratives) there emerged these ruptures. Hoss, Little Joe, and *papá* Ben (Lorne Greene) stepped up to right racist wrongs. And Manolito functioned as a bridge between communities. We are in a #browntv twenty-first-century epoch and we don't have this kind of radical TV.

Bill: No, you are SO right: the complexity is absent—when I was trying to get my own TV series launched a couple of years ago (a tragic tale of Hollywood catastrophes that goes by the name of *Mextasy*), I happened to meet up with Norman Lear, whose seventies oeuvre of social-justice-advocacy comedies changed the face of the nation in the years after the 1960s : *All in the Family* (1971–79), *Sanford and Son* (1972–77), *Maude* (1972–78), *Good Times* (1974–79), et cetera. It was a brief encounter, but I was thrilled, as I got to tell him to his face how much his shows impacted my mind and my life and how much, in a way that I hadn't even countenanced to that moment, the "syntax" of these shows suffused my imagination.

Fede: *Pistoleros* occupy an outergalactic spatial imaginary, too. I think of Lorne Greene as our bridge from tellurian frontiersman doing the right thing to galactic *paterfamilia* in *Battlestar Galactica* (1978–79) and *Galactica* (1980). While the eighties show didn't feature Latinxs per se, its 2000 makeover, *Battlestar Galactica* (2003–9), and prequel, *Caprica* (2010), did—and in spades.

Bill: And with *Zoot Suit* (1981) Chicano-god-of-actors Edward James Olmos instead of Lorne Greene!

Fede: Yes, we get our very own zoot-suiter in space with Olmos's role as Admiral William Adama in the reboot of *Battlestar Galactica.* Here he's a great rhetor, strategist, leader of the people, and savior of a new generation of existence: the human-cylon Hera. As Fabio Chee writes, "The premise of *Battlestar Galactica* is that the surviving population of a faraway system of planets comes to Earth to populate it during what we identify as 'prehistory.' This element suggests that the population of the ship is, thus, pre-racialized and this is explained by the show's insistence on promoting post-racial environments in which race seems to have ambiguous historical value."[6] And, as we learn from the prequel, Ronald D. Moore's *Caprica* (2010), the Adamas are Taurons (coded as Latinxs). Indeed, it is William Adama who ultimately settles his lost tribe on the planet that will be known as Earth. In *Caprica,* William Adama's a boy; his single father's Joseph Adama, played by yet another of our iconic eighties actors, Esai Morales.

Remember him as the tough older brother, Bob, in Luis Valdez's *La Bamba* 1987? The young William Adama grows up on Caprica, where he endures interplanetary racism and bigotry: the Taurons are called stinking dirt-eaters by the Capricans (coded as white, rational: civilization). In spite of the overt racism he experiences, William finds refuge in the language of home (code-switching between English, Hebrew, and Spanish), rituals (death of a family member), family lineage celebrated through tattoo art, and home-cooked meals. For Fabio Chee, *Caprica* does "more for Latinas/os and other minorities than any other science fiction show on television to date. This is demonstrated by the insistence on detailing ethnic and racial discrimination and how tradition combats them."[7] The show "pushes its audience to recognize that racism still exists."[8]

Bill: I love that it is Olmos around which all this backstory in *Caprica* is being engineered to justify—the king of West Coast theater with his *Pachuco* role in *Zoot Suit*; a life-changing educator in *Stand and Deliver* (1988); and, for me, his most outsized and underrated role as a *cholo barrio vato,* Montoya

Santana, in *American Me,* a film Olmos also directed—he would not get a directing gig for a decade after that searing film—an evocation of barrio/homoerotic violence that no one knew what to do with!

And, of course, his sly, silent ubiquity as a biracial Asian in *Blade Runner.*

Fede: Before we turn our gaze to *Blade Runner* (1982) and its deep etching into the Latinx imaginary, let me mention another sci-fi show that imagines us in the future: CBS's *Star Trek: Discovery* (2017–). It had the social media universe all a-twitter when Bryan Fuller (of *American Gods*) and Alex Kurtzman cast gay Blatinx actor Wilson Cruz (he played Latinx-queer avant-la-TV-lettre Enrique "Rickie" Vasquez in ABC's mid-nineties *My So-Called Life*) as the gay Dr. Hugh Culber.

Bill: God, you watch a lot of television! I am barely caught up with *Stranger Things* (no Latinx folks in the Upside Down, not even in season 3). But, yes, Mr. Cruz has caught my eye of late—especially in the *Huff Post* interview where he shares how

> as a fan of the franchise, I count myself among the countless LGBTQ fans who have longed to see themselves and our relationships depicted on *Star Trek* . . . The fact is that we have always been here, but finally seeing ourselves and our stories included in this, truly, American mythology confirms what we've always known to be true—which is that we are an integral part of this culture and we always will be.[9]

Fede: And here I have a confession to make. Excited to see how a gay Latinx space explorer might exist on prime-time TV, I binge-watched the entire first season of *Star Trek: Discovery*. Fuller's writing against the genre (as one would expect given the radical innovation he fleshes out in *American Gods*) was elastic and exhilarating. And the casting of a woman of color (Sonequa Martin-Green, also in *The Walking Dead*) as the maverick, outlaw Starfleet explorer Michael Burnham is a breath of fresh air. She's smart (Vulcan smart). She's a badass warrior. She's African American.

However, the narrative trips and tumbles when it comes to Latinx—queer and straight. They cast British Jason Isaacs as Captain *Gabriel Lorca* (huh?). And, by giving Wilson Cruz's character a French-sounding last name, they make "color-blind" and erase any Latinx that might have informed his role as Dr. Culber. Moreover, it takes the narrative till episode 4 to begin to subtly suggest that Culber and his partner, astronomycologist Paul Stamets (Anthoy Rapp), are a gay couple. It isn't till the end of episode 5 (53 minutes into the show) that we see them together in the bathroom brushing their teeth, talking, and gently touching one another.

While most of the episodes don't feature Culber and Stamets together (and when they do appear together, it's only for a minute or less), episode 9 does something rather bold: Stamets tells Culber: "I love you." Culber reciprocates with the same. The episode features the two actually kissing—and in medium close-up. So, if we take the fact that *Modern Family* has yet to show the instantiation of interracial and intergenerational romance (Gloria and Jay), then *Star Trek: Discovery*'s way ahead of the game.

Going back in time, I was thirteen when Ridley Scott's *Blade Runner* (1982) was released. It was one of those films I snuck in to see with my mischievous compadres Miguel and Brian. We'd paid to see a matinee of *E.T. the Extra-*

Terrestrial (1982) but instead grabbed seats in the adjacent R-rated *Blade Runner*. I'd never imagined anything like this could be done in cinema. Scott's spectacularly conceived storyworld was total—and, as you mention, it included our very own smooth-moving, wise, and taciturn officer Gaff (Olmos), who leaves paper trails of origami animal figurines.

Gaff's words leave more of an impression than the monologues of Deckard (Harrison Ford) and Roy (Rutger Hauer). He tells Deckard: "It's too bad [Rachel] won't live. But then again, who does." Scott's prescience foretells of a future—*our* now—where the 1 percent Anglo *haves*, like Tyrell, live in high-tech pyramids, and the 99 percent multiracial *have-nots* live in the streets with Asian and Mex-tech taco trucks. Through his visual mixture of architectures (mesoamerican, Asian, you name it) and high-tech gadgetry (flying cars), Scott extrapolates from his 1980 reality a world that depicts clear-cut class differences based on race, and with the cultural hybridity and mashup he conveys the *unevenness* in social, technical, and economic development.

Gaff embodies this admixture. He's an ethnoracial and cultural hybrid that bridges the world of the haves with the have-nots—in this case, the Replicants *qua* slaves like Roy (Rutger Hauer), who at the end of the film tells Deckard: "It's quite an experience to live in fear. That's what it is to be a slave." The *pachuco* Gaff is the go-between; it's his presence that collapses class divisions and allows knowledge to pass from hunted (Roy) to hunter (Deckard). Gaff not only indirectly brokers this epistemological exchange, he himself is the repository of knowledge. As *Blade Runner* comes to a close, it's Gaff's words that echo loud and that ambiguate Deckard's ontology: is he human or android, and does it matter? Science fiction, as noted Chicana critic Catherine Ramírez reminds, "can prompt us to recognize and rethink the status quo by depicting an alternative world, be it a parallel universe, distant future, or revised past."[10] For Ramírez, science fiction "tweaks what we take to be reality or history and in doing so exposes its constructedness."[11]

Denis Villeneuve's *Blade Runner 2049* (2017) features Olmos as an aged Gaff. But with Disney's Ryan Gosling all grown up and pretty, he steals the limelight, sweeping our *pachuco* (and race and ethnicity generally) into the mise-en-scène shadows.

Bill: Later we are going to have to deal more with Latinx actors as avatars of a nefarious species of next-generation evil, so I am happy to frolic here in science fiction where, perhaps still, hope still can thrive.

Fede: HBO's *Westworld* (2017–) is all about robots (from *roboti,* which derives from the Old Church Slavanic *rabota,* or servitude)—ethnic and racially identified robots that turn against their white British master, apotheosized by Anthony Hopkins in his role as Dr. Robert Ford. Jonathan Nolan (yes, another

Nolan for us to talk about) and Lisa Joy cast Clifton Collins Jr. (grandson of the legendary Pedro Gonzalez Gonzalez) as gunslinging Latinx outlaw robot Lawrence. They cast Rodrigo Santoro as Latinx cowboy womanizer robot Hector Escatón, who wakes to his servitude and speciesism, helping lead the robot revolution.

Bill: I just can't get over the repetition compulsion enacted at the beginning of every episode (sometimes twice in the same episode) which announces like an optical refrain the pursuit of a Latino bandit as a key element of the show / series. It's as if the showrunners are giving the point: that the Western, as a genre, in the past, in the present, and in the future, must needs feature Mexicanesque banditry as a keynote, as the foundation of the Western itself. We just can't escape it: Mexicans and Latinxs (as Hollywood is not particular) as wanted—owing to an intrinsic criminality—and as with *want*, creatures of abject poverty, propertyless, undocumented and in need of eviction.

Fede: We've had some other instances of sci-fi in the constructing of a #browntv imaginary. There was Evan Katz's *The Event* (2010–11) that featured the Afro-Latino Cuban American president Elias Martinez (played by Blair Underwood) as he battles humanlike illegally residing aliens. In episode 15, "Face Off," Martinez gives the green light to blow up the "aliens"—symbolically tied to Latinxs through the casting of the aforementioned Clifton Collins Jr. as

Thomas. In other words, in this Brown televisually imagined postrace US, the Blatinx president doesn't stand in solidarity with the aliens (aka Latinxs); he forces the aliens (Latinxs) to blow themselves up. Postrace US is Latinxs versus Latinxs.

As you brought up earlier in our *conversación*, Bill, the representation of Latinxs in sci-fi is even more rich and complicated in the hands and imagination of the Latinx film director Alex Rivera. We see in *Sleep Dealer* (2008) how global capitalists use advances in technology to exploit Mexican *braceros*, forcing them to work longer hours and without having to cross the border; without having to sully the US. Rivera constructs a film that portrays how the automatized Latinx borderland subject represents the reality of a brown-body labor force that is made to see itself as a machine.

Bill: For me, Alex Rivera's *Sleep Dealer* is one of these visual cultural viral agents. It's a flash of progressive *transmogrifications* in the Brown image repertoire. On the surface, the film is a cool sci-fi flick about hackers, hacking, work, workers, and migration at the US–Mexico border. However, hidden within the synapses (can a film have a synapse?) of its sequences we see it is a meditation on subjectivity in the twenty-first century.

Fede: Rivera invites his audience to synaptically jack-in—an audience that's Latinx. Once the synaptic arcing begins, we as the audience experience a deeply prescient political critique of today's exploitation of Latinxs—and also the US's control over water rights that determine the fates of families in Mexico. He also leaves us with signs (material and imaginary) pointing toward a better tomorrow: Memo Cruz (Luis Fernando Peña) shares his story as he plants seeds that grow a new crop after a newly politically woke Rudy Ramirez (Jacob Vargas) uses drone technology to blow up a corporate-controlled dam (Del Rio Water) that gives water back to the Mexican *gente.*

Bill: Most memorable in *Sleep Dealer* is the collaboration in the end between the *Mexican National,* Memo Cruz, and the *Mexican American* Rudy Ramirez— just the appearance of this commonplace (in the Southland) differentiation in a feature film was enough to knock me off my feet. Later, meeting and speaking with Rivera, it was brought home to me just how hard it is to communicate this nuance to an audience weaned on the typical binaries, good guys versus bad guys, white versus dark, et cetera. Rivera's film forces viewers into the myriad reverberations of race, history, politics, and eros that are afoot at/in/on the US–Mexico border.[12] Rashida Jones's "Nosedive" in the third season of *Black Mirror,* focused on an Anglo-American's fetishization of her social media score, is actually a silent meditation on race and black lives not mattering in the near future. Both Jones and Rivera are to be championed for bringing their visions to television.

Fede: Rivera's *Sleep Dealer* along with his shorts like *A Robot Walks into a Bar* (2014) or *Why Cybraceros?* (http://alexrivera.com/) add to and expand a corpus that now includes US Latinos like Robert Rodriguez (*Planet Terror,* 2007) but also increasingly those from south of the border. I think of Carlos Salces's *Zurdo* (Mexico, 2003), Rodrigo Ordóñez Nischli's *Depositarios* (Mexico, 2010), Francisco Laresgoiti's *2033* (Mexico, 2009), Esteban Sapir's *La antena* (Argentina, 2007), Diego Ayala's *Conexión* (Chile, 2013), and Fernando Meirelles's *Blindness* (Brazil, 2008). That is, Rivera uses digital technology and the internet to create, with a small budget, movies that we view online and that expand the periodic table of independent, world science fiction narratives. He's part of a Latinx gen of filmmakers with access to twenty-first-century technologies that earlier Latino filmmakers didn't have.

Have you seen, too, what Rivera does with his installation pieces that also use digital platforms and the internet to wake audiences to Latinx existence today? Take, for instance, Rivera's installations, "Memorial Over General Atomics" and "Lowdrone," first physically exhibited at UC San Diego, which continue to live at http://alexrivera.com.

Rivera takes a technology of surveillance and destruction (drones used to monitor the US–Mexico border *and,* in their scaled-up versions, drop bombs), strips it down and reconstructs it with new parts—and with a new use: as a cultural object for us to apprehend and to make sense of today's reality *and* with a new use function. With his "Memorial" repurposed drone he creates an aerial sculpture that combines drone technology with human radial bones. He asks us not only to fly with this repurposed and re-missioned drone to see what is happening at the factory where they create drones of mass destruction,

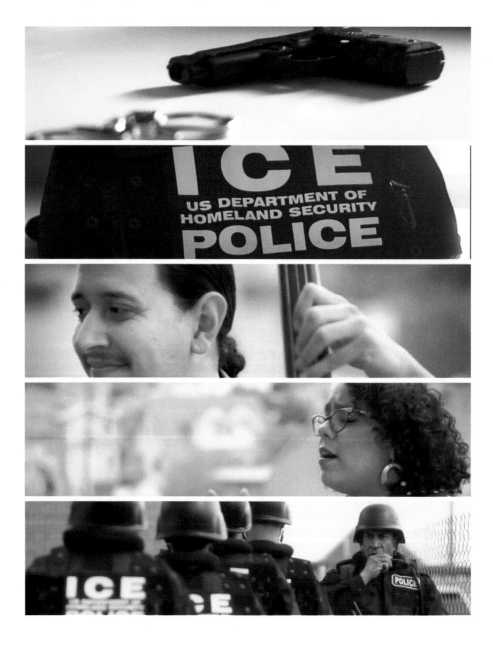

but also to think about the radial bones that function to hold its propellers: the laboring arm (or *bracero*) worked to death. Rivera's repurposing of the drone in "Lowdrone" similarly asks us to establish a new relationship with the use function of a tech-object otherwise used for destruction. Here Rivera combines a model of a vintage lowrider (kicking its wheels out to the edges as blades to a repurposed drone) that one can use to watch the surveyor (*la migra*) as one flies or "hops" back and forth across the wall that divides Mexico (Tijuana) from the US (San Ysidro).

Bill: I am more familiar with Rivera's efforts in music videos. His work with La Santa Cecilia, a progressive group of musicians/artists from Los Angeles—the band, including Marisol "La Marisoul" Hernandez, Jose "Pepe" Carlos, Miguel "Oso" Ramirez, and Alex Bendana, teamed up with Alex Rivera to film "El Hielo (ICE)," a music video featuring undocumented actors and activists.

The music video, produced in 2013, part of the #Not1More series at http://notonemoredeportation.com, tells a daily tale of tragedy from our American Southwestern sector—as with *Sleep Dealer,* Rivera is careful to document the complexity of our daily Californian realities with Latinx perpetrators filling the role of ICE agents and prey, the undocumented masses of surplus labor enabling the robust economies of the US's most prosperous state.

Fede: They move us out of his Latinxfuturity mode and into our present day—but then again, isn't Latinxfuturity an extrapolation of today? Certainly, his music videos are a far cry from J-Lo's "I Luh Ya Papí." In an interview I did with Rivera I talk about how his music videos round out his *"Transfrontera-*

Latinx aesthetic."[13] Rivera's camera eye puts the spotlight on *banda,* soul, and rock 'n' roll soundscapes formed from musicians hailing from all parts of the Américas: La Santa Cecilia, Aloe Blacc, Manu Chau, and Ana Tijoux. However, Rivera's soundscapes work as a palimpsestic overlay to visuals that depict the struggles of real-life day laborers, activists, and family members of deported immigrants. In her analysis of two such music videos, "El Hielo (ICE)" and "Wake Me Up," Rebecca Schreiber demonstrates how Rivera's careful camera work and point-of-view lensing and editing visually convey the subjectivity of "migrant apprehension and its effects on the everyday lives of undocumented Latina/os."[14] That is, Rivera uses filmic visual shaping devices to create a camera presence that travels *with* the migrant workers, and not one that looks and judges from above or from afar.

So, while at first sound, one might think of these as conventional music videos that feature artists like Tijoux and Manu Chau, on a second look, the auditory (music and lyrics) create a contrapuntal play with the visuals of everyday life for Latinxs surviving at the edges of society. Rivera asks his audience to carry both sights and sounds in mind. He asks us to see the ways in which musical lyrics and sounds by activist artists like Tijoux and Manu Chau can intensify but not sentimentalize understanding of the undocumented, detained, and deported.

Bill: I can watch Ana Tijoux's "Shock in Arizona" video again and again and again. A moving, cool collaboration with the National Day Laborer Organizing Network, the National Immigrant Youth Alliance and Puente Movement, with music by Tijoux and lensed by Lisa Renzler with Rivera directing, "Shock in Arizona" is a compelling fusion of earthy rhythms and down and brown, agit-prop community resistance. The YouTube posting of the video liner notes adds how Tijoux "is the latest artist to lend her support in Arizona as part of the 'Alto Arizona,' a campaign focused on the visibility, respect and dignity for immigrants that have been the target of hate and criminalization not only in Arizona but around the world."

There is a calm, somewhat surreal, feel in the video's opening movement, with Tijoux in the Arizona desert backed only by a drummer on a beatbox and a guitarist—to her left sit four Latinx activists holding a sheet onto which photos of Sheriff Joe Arpaio (aka Ar*payaso,* Ar-clown), Arizona, and riot cops are projected. Tijoux's lyrics are a call to arms, and the mise-en-scène of the video emerges as an invocation, a call to action that is just not part of your typical Drake video.

Fede: While on the topic of music videos, we'd be seriously remiss if we didn't mention the glorious epoch of MTV and how it shaped #browntv sensibilities. Four years after the launch of MTV, NBC began airing its prime-time #browntv series, *Miami Vice* (1984–90). The show not only features Eddie Olmos as Martin "Marty" Castillo (he becomes the vice squad's lieutenant in season 1, episode 6, "One Eyed Jack"), it also launched Jimmy Smits's acting career. In the pilot, he's cast as Crockett's (Don Johnson) first partner (before Ricardo "Rico" Tubbs), Eddie Rivera, before he's blown up (season 1, episode 1, "Brother's Keeper," September 16, 1984).

Bill: What a show—you know, that's my big fear about writing this book: leaving out key players in the pantheon of #browntv. That's why we are going to maintain a Facebook and Instagram page, and use the #browntv hashtag so that our readers can help us write the sequel to this exchange. But back to *Miami Vice*—what an epic! With Edward James Olmos, Philip Michael Thomas, Saundra Santiago, and Olivia Brown starring, backed up by token gringos (;-o) Don Johnson, John Diehl, and Michael Talbott, the show blazed a Technicolor/pastel trail that introduced new hues to national TV—and I am not just talking about the wild colors of Miami, with its Cuban, Haitian, and Caribbean palettes, I am talking about the racialized mix of a Miami (including its substantial barrios filled with Jewish American retirees) that complicated the view of an America, a US, only then on the brink of its racist, antimulticultural present.

Fede: Indeed, in our retrograde racist mediated present the #browntv of the eighties is looking better and better. We mentioned earlier J-Lo as Harlee Santos in NBC's current DEA-centered televisual narrative *Shades of Blue* (January 2016–). Sure, we have a Latina protagonist on prime-time TV, but *how* is she the protagonist. The creators of the show depict her as duplicitous, a traitor, and a murderer. They write her within the most stereotyped and patriarchal (à la Octavio Paz) version of *la malinche* / *malintzin*—and not Anzaldúa's strategic reclamation of our ur-*mamá*. Harlee's one of a long list of Latina *mamás* on TV (past and present) who seem to exist only as double-crossers willing to sacrifice their progeny.

Bill: Oh, now you have me yearning for the earnest *Chicanito* wonder that was Fernando Vásquez as baby Jesus–stealing Paco Mendoza in the December 21, 1967, episode of *Dragnet* on NBC. Bill Koenig's synopsis captures the tale in all its awesomeness:

> Friday and Gannon investigate the theft of a statue of the baby Jesus from a church's nativity scene on Christmas Eve. The figure itself has little monetary

value. Father Xavier Rojas explains this Jesus statue has been at the church for decades and has great sentimental value to the parishioners. The detectives pursue a lead but come up empty. As they return to Father Rojas, a small boy is pulling a wagon with the statue in it. The boy had prayed for a new wagon and promised the baby Jesus the first ride if he received it. The episode is a remake of "The Big Little Baby Jesus" from the original series, with three cast members (in addition to Jack Webb) reprising their original roles.[15]

The episode was a remake of "The Big Little Jesus" (1953), on the original black-and-white *Dragnet*. Am I just nostalgic for loving this apparition of #brownTV in the middle of the sixties on the most conservative show in the US, *Dragnet*? It's funny because Jack "Clean Cut, Just the Facts" Webb is whispered to be either Jewish or Native American, or both, which further muddles the scene.

And isn't that just what we need from television? More of the muddle, more of the mix, more of the mess that is America, the most fantabulous experiment in nationhood? The "land of the free" but built on the capital of slaves, the surplus value of an almost incarcerated working class? Paco is your typical thieving Mexican, ultimately, but the downhome warmth of his intent baptizes us with a different kind of water. I am a recovering Catholic, but there is something in the mextasy of this that makes me shiver!

Fede: Paco got his wagon and Jesus, and with it #browntv spins its imaginary of prepubescent Latinxs who teeter at the edge of innocent naiveté and dastardly derring-do. And this increasingly becomes embodied, well, in phenotypically marked bodies: lighter-skinned = good versus browner-skinned = bad. Think of light-skinned Demi Lovato or Selena Gomez (as children in *Barney & Friends* (1992–2010) then teens in any number of Disney Channel shows) coded as good, assimilated Latinas. Then think Demi Lovato's half-sister, Madison De La Garza, who plays Juanita Solis, daughter of the hot-

tempered and oversexed Gabi and Carlos Solis, in *Desperate Housewives*, where the show (largely through her Latina *mamá,* Gabi) codes her as bad, abnormal: overweight.

As we move through the Brown televisual imaginary into teenhood, think of the darker-skinned Naya Rivera as bad, lesbian Latina Santana, in *Glee* (2009–15).

Bill: Naya Rivera as Santana! Is she *bad* because she is swarthy, or swarthy because she is *bad*? And lesbian—that's the kicker, right? Latinas since Lupe Velez are, pardon the Derrida syntax, always already sexually deviant, erotically charged, preternaturally prone to a species of *amor* that is somehow eccentric to a cis-nation's normed covetous appetite for heterosexual affections. It is as if her lesbian longings coupled with her dark-skin DNA sentence her from the start.

And her late 2017 headlines, from "real life / reel life" (post *TMZ*, it's all the same) won't do anything to erode these tropes or eat away at these stereotypes: "Naya Rivera Charged with Domestic Battery After Alleged Altercation with Husband Ryan Dorsey" and "Husband Says Actress Naya Rivera 'Is Out of Control' in 911 Call after Domestic Battery Incident." In the end, "thank goodness she's straight" is complemented by "OMG—she's a wild, violent, Latina!"[16] Of course, shortly thereafter hubby Ryan Dorsey dropped all charges.

And then there is Michelle Rodriguez . . .

Fede: Michelle Rodriguez as the badass Shé in *Machete* is Naya Rivera all grown up. And while Rodriguez lensed and spliced a *reel* Latinx imaginary that turned Manichean codings upside down, it seems from the *People* magazine story and newsfeed you just cited that the *real* Naya Rivera's doing this in everyday life with her domestic battery rap-sheet.[17]

I have to say I'm on her side. Don't mess with Naya.

Bill: Your mention of "Manichean" sent me on one more trip to Douglas Harper's amazing etymological word DNA machine:

> Manicheism 1550s, "the religion of the Manichees" (late 14c.) a Gnostic Christian sect named for its founder, *Mani* (Latin Manichæus), c.215–275, Syriac-speaking apostle from a Jesus cult in Mesopotamia in 240s, who taught a universal religion. Vegetarian and visionary, they saw "particles of light and goodness" trapped in evil matter and regarded Satan as co-eternal with God. The universe was a scene of struggle between good and evil. The sect was characterized by dualism and a double-standard of perfectionist "elects" and a larger group of fellow travelers who would require several reincarnations before their particles of light would be liberated.[17]

Couple that with this little image from my graphic rovings . . .

Mani, the prophet—an image, in the public domain, from
Guillermo Nericcio García's digital archive. File: Mani.jpg
From Wikimedia Commons, the free media repository,
https://commons.wikimedia.org/wiki/File:Mani.jpg.

. . . and I think old Mani would enjoy our cultural incarceration, our semi-otic (and semi-idiotic paralysis) as we bounce between worlds good (white, untanned, calm, within the law) and worlds swarthy (cue the dark sex, baby; the evil looks; the cross-the-street-as-I-am-scared 'realities').

Fede: Bill, I think this is our cue to move to our next section of the book, "From Niños and Teens to Comidas."

From *Niños* and Teens
to *Comidas*

Fede: Many of our generation grew up with Saturday-morning cartoons. We didn't have TV at home, but our *abuelita* did—and one of those cathode-ray beasts carved into some serious piece of oak furniture.

I loved my *abuelita*, Alicia. I loved her TV more. Friday-night sleepovers would land me on her plastic-covered couch—a trademark of older gen. Latinx households, *¿que no?*—for some serious Saturday-morning gluttony: a large bowl of fluorescent multicolored (radioactive?) Trix and Saturday-

morning cartoons. I remember when El Dorado in *The Super Friends* (1981) caught my eye. I couldn't believe my eyes and ears: a Latino superhero in cartoons. Later, I'd become aware of just how sloppy ABC's creative team was in their construction of El Dorado: a hodgepodge of cultural references and anachronisms, including the willy-nilly juxtaposing of name (El Dorado as mythic Peruvian city of gold) with a gold-laden, hieroglyphed, wide-collar neck and chest piece that features the Mexican symbol of the eagle.

Bill: An odd claim to fame (and infamy), my work in the ivory tower (and beyond) is associated with all manner of manufactured, invented, fabulous, and ersatz "Mexicans." My first book, *Tex[t]-Mex: Seductive Hallucinations of the "Mexican" in America,* does its best to analyze (and, in some cases, vivisect) all manner of invented Latinxs prowling around the infotainment corridors of the Americas—from Speedy Gonzalez and Charlton Heston (Vargas! in Orson Welles's *Touch of Evil*) to Salma Hayek and Rita Hayworth (born Margarita Carmen Cansino, but not even "Mexican" at all, being of Spanish and Irish pedigree). So, collecting (I say it is *curating* not *hoarding*) Mexicanesque and Latina/o artifacts takes up tons of my time and crowds most of the alleyways of my imagination. Case in point and utterly coincidental, as it seems we share a fetish for this *mezcla* man of Mesoamerican confusion, El Dorado!

A B-star, to be sure, in the stable of ABC's *Super Friends* (1980–82; think *The Justice League of America* with hyper foul and cheap limited-animation, aka *crapimation*), El Dorado never appeared in a real *bona fide* comic book—instead, he was an add-on walk-on for DC's Saturday-morning superhero drama. Take it away, *wikiworldia*: "El Dorado was created solely for the *Super Friends* cartoons and has never appeared in a DC Comic. He first appeared as a minor character in animated shorts that aired in the 1981 season and later in *Super Friends: The Legendary Super Powers Show* as a full-time member. El Dorado spoke English with an accent, sporadically substituting common Spanish words or phrases, such as adding words like 'rápido' and replacing nearly every instance of 'yes' with 'sí.'" Imagine some peculiar, misbegotten, animated grandfather of *Dora the Explorer* and you've got the right picture.

Debate rages regarding his superpowers, but they seem to be limited to teleportation and projection using the magic of his lovely red cape. He's no Superman; El Dorado's main power seems to be his Mexican accent, his uncanny ability to disappear, and, for ABC at the time, tap into the growing "Hispanic" demographic. My current goal is to add El Dorado, the Super Friend plastic action figure / ersatz "Mexican," to my traveling Mextasy exhibition / museum pop-up show / circus of *desmadres*. If any of you out there reading this run across him at some auction, swap meet, or trash can, do please write me at memo@sdsu.edu—the cash reward I send you will make your head spin!

Fede: Cartoons weren't my only exposure to #browntv early on. I also recall identifying with those differently marked subjects that made up the Addams Family (1964–66). I actually thought they were Latinx. They all had black hair like my family. They existed at the margins of society.

Bill: Ha! Maybe my obsession with *Heckle and Jeckle* cartoons was a subterranean longing for trickster dark subjectivities—some prescient blend of Skip Gates's *Signifying Monkey* and *The Cartoon Network*. Most memorable? From 1951, "Bulldozing the Bull," directed by Eddie Donnelly, this Terrytoons classic finds Heckle and Jeckle in Mexico paired off against an angry bull.

Some of the Zorro tropes weave their way into the featurette, as you can see here.

Fede: Nascent experiences with a #browntv imaginary began even before my *chicaspatas* carried me from Mexico into the US. Born and diapered in Mexico City, I sucked at the teat of *Cri-Cri* (*el grillito cantor*) and *El Chapulín Colorado*. To this day, an image of this crazed dude, Roberto Gomez Bolaños as Chespirito, who never seemed to shed his pajamas, transports me to this pre-US–Mexico-border-crossing early life. The sounds and images of *Cri-Cri* and *Chapulín Colorado* burrowed deep into my brain. That, and the smells of *panaderías* with its fresh-baked *pan dulces* . . . You can take the brown body outta Mexico, but never Mexico outta the brown body.

Bill: You are taking me back—it is 1966, and I am sitting with my father in his room—he is smoking Tareytons and drinking Schlitz beer. I sit and watch mesmerized as he flips between the channels day to day. One minute we are watching Raúl Velasco, Mexico's Johnny Carson; the next

we are watching Johnny Carson, the US's Raúl Velasco.

El Chapulin Colorado is there, but not that often—with my daddy, it's wrestling, and his favorite fighter Mil Mascaras chasing down Wahoo McDaniel in the ring—I know, I know, I already alluded to them above, but I can't get them out of my head. All these memories are in black-and-white, Spanish and English, the wash of memory and aroma—my dad, his beer, the cigarettes. . . . The beauty of it all—my synapses infused with a bilingual and bicultural immersion courtesy of an old RCA TV and rabbit-eared antennas.

Fede: We're addicts, Bill. It's the mainlining of #browntv opioids that transport us to those halcyon days of childhood—Schlitz and all. Indeed, you're the twenty-first-century curator—*pusherman*—of such visionquest-inducing Brown ephemera. But not all #browntv's up to the challenge, as we've made clear thus far in our conjoint odyssey. You and your *papá*'s bonding over Mil Mascaras has today become a silver-screen toxin. Think Jerrod Hess's mangling up of *lucha*

libre into pure buffoonery with *Nacho Libre* (2006), creating deeper lines of division that exclude more than envelop and that include Jack Black in Brownface (priest by day and luchador by night) along with Hector Jimenez as his droopy-lipped (literally) Latino sidekick, Esqueleto, getting the laughs—but not from Latinxs.

The same with the cartoon character you mention in the same breath as El Dorado, Dora, along with her *bandido* sidekick, Swiper. *Dora the Explorer* (and now she's a tween) is Latina, but again a reconstruction that's aimed for non-Latinx audiences. (I cringe when imagining what damage will be done to #brownlatinidad when British director James Bobin releases to the world his *reel* action adventure flick, *Dora and the Lost City of Gold.* Its potential saving grace: the casting of one our great Latinx actors, Michael Peña, as the *papá.*) Dora teaches kids Spanish-isms, but like Handy Manny, it's language without cultural content. It's *functional* Spanish. How to ask your handy Latinx if they can fix your tire or pick your fruit or clean your house. It's #browntv that crashes us down hard from our opioid highs.

I'm in desperate need of an injection, Bill.

Bill: Fede! You're a real Debbie Downer—but you are right of course. As Dora the Explorer morphs into a tween, she becomes ever more mall-ready, ever more the perfect consumer. And as you can see here, you can watch her on TV or "play her" (be her) via video games—or, as you mention, see her in live-action adventure flicks!

"Dora and Friends: Into the City" debuts! And then, what's next? "Dora, the Sad College Years?" Never one to say no to a good thing, Nickelodeon opts to cash in on their Latina golden goose! Instead of "Swiper, No Swiping," we get Dora the Explorer all grown up, ten years old, hangin' with her posse in the City, and, get this, now she has eyebrows. But then, I am actually all for the saturation of the vidiot network with pint-sized facsimiles of smart, bilingual, Latina animated stars, so I was able to hold my snark for a minute till I happened to click on the curriculum/lesson plan Nickelodeon shoved out along with their would-be Latinx tween star.

Well-meaning, noble, and detailed, it's enough to make you burn your TV!

DORA AND FRIENDS CURRICULUM

Dora and Friends extends Dora the Explorer's play-along interactive format through music and interactive songs.

Dora & Friends Curriculum

Interpersonal, intrapersonal, linguistic skills, and so much more is what your child is developing every time you tune into "Dora and Friends!" Find out how your child is growing in each area.

Fede: With Dora the tween, tykes are now officially slumming it in a sterile *Stepford Wives*–styled, content-evacuated "Latinidad"—with heavy *heavy* quotation marks. Thank the gods for *El Tigre* (2007–8)—a show that got traction right around when Corina was learning to take her first steps and that

provided me with that much-needed injection. I loved its flash-animation movements and color palette; it was so unlike the unremarkable pastels of *Dora*. It was #browntv that affirmed our Latinx identities. It was cartoon storyspace anchored in our culture. The high was short-lived. *El Tigre* was canceled, and *Dora* kept on going.

Bill: For me, the injection was the early madness of *The Powerpuff Girls* (1998–2005)—a series I watched with Lorenzo and Sophia when they were growing up in the late nineties and early aughts. Jorge R. Gutierrez and Sandra Equihua's *El Tigre: The Adventures of Manny Rivera* creates a universe filled with visual cacophony, a chaos of mad Latinx colors and stylings that dazzled the eyes and provoked the imagination. *El Tigre,* like Craig McCracken's *The Powerpuff Girls,* provided an oasis of amphetamine-laced (I am speaking of the pace/tempo here) narrative—the perfect narrative vehicles to prepare that generation for the iPads and smartphones that were to emerge just around the corner.

We are focused on nationality and ethnicity, but the old Marxist in me says we also have to think about class when we think about what we see and what we don't see on the glorious boob tube. Back in 2011 *Sesame Street* producers were busy patting themselves on the back for introducing a hungry, impoverished (homeless?) character named Lily—here, wow, now, in 2011, something is being done. But back in the day it was commonplace to see poor, streetwise Mexican "youth" clowning their way through having nothing on *El Chavo del Ocho* (1971–80)—a show whose puns and wordplay prepared me for the syntactic shenanigans of Julio Cortázar and Vladimir Nabokov.[1] And *Sanford and Son*'s old junkyard, glossed above, allowed me to get down and dirty (and laugh) with the working poor.

In 2017, it strikes me that all this is gone. And when it comes to the poor, homeless, and impoverished, I go back to my early work on Speedy Gonzales animated features from Warner Brothers—there the mise-en-scène almost always includes #browntv subjectivities living in the trash.

Fede: We keep bungee-jumping back in time, Bill. Speedy—a subject near and dear to you as *the* Speedologist—along with *Sesame Street*'s Latinx character-actors were indeed the spaces I sutured my imagination to.

No matter how many times he says *Ándale! ¡Ándale! ¡Arriba! ¡Arriba! ¡Epa! ¡Epa! ¡Epa! Yeehaw!* and no matter how outlandish and racist is his *charro* garb, I love the Speedster.

Enlighten me. Is it because in the end he's the smartest and most agile of them all, Daffy to Sylvester included? Is it that he's our only brown savior in a sea of white messiahs? How is this possible given that he's just as much a stereotype as D. W. Griffith's worst of the worst—or that crazy Don Pedro monolith at the South Carolina theme park "South of the Border."

Bill: For one, we know he is not "Mexican"—not even "Mexicanesque." The brainchild of Isadore "Yitzak" "Friz" Freleng and Robert McKimson, and mouthed by Mel Blanc, Speedy Gonzales continues to triumph in our imaginations for multiple reasons: he is a success (he wins! Outsmarting East Coast Gringo Pussy *Gato* Sylvester with his thieving wily mind and gifted speed). He's also a rake, he's good "with the ladies," so that from a Darwinian point of view, we (cis-*fixed* being the "norm"), we (or "we") happily embrace his rascally romantic prowess. Last, it's a fucking desert out there for Latinx subjectivities scouring the networks and streams in search of themselves. Remember, entertainment is a mirror—even before we all started carrying electronic mirrors and cameras, it was to the screen that we ran for existential succor. *Arriba Arriba*—the homonymics of Spanish, even Mel Blanc's aural simulacra of the same, somehow soothes the savage beast!

Fede: Mostly, what we see in today's animation is the same old, same old: the brown folks helping clean up messes left by white folks, and the white folks getting all the glory. Remember Pixar's *Turbo* (2013)? Well, it's the Latinxs that help Turbo, an otherwise impossibly slow snail (voiced by Ryan Reynolds) win the race—and save the day. What were they thinking? I mean, the narrative is set in the San Fernando Valley—a place where Latinxs are the clear majority. Yet, it's the white guy (snail in this case) who's still the savior at the end of the day. And, in *Cloudy with a Chance of Meatballs* (2009) it is the Latinx Juan-of-all-trades, Manny, who helps the entrepreneurial white protagonist, Flint Lockwood, save the day. In *Cars* (2006), Ramone plays the sidekick to the Anglo-identified McQueen (voiced by Owen Wilson), who wins the day.

Even in the world of animation where creators can go anywhere, they are straightjacketed by the *Dances with Wolves,* white-savior mentality.

Bill: The worst of all was *A Bug's Life,* also from Pixar (1998). John Lasseter and Andrew Stanton re-vivify all metonymies associated with Mexicans, detritus, laziness, and banditry, as a sombrero becomes a floating signifier of cantina-existentia for criminality and a hangout for marauding grasshoppers.

That Kevin Spacey as Hopper gives his annihilate-the-ant's speech from this context accomplishes two things at once: the sombrero is old, torn, and dirty; but it also is the tropic embodiment of menacing Mexican banditry.

Nice trick, Pixar!

Fede: *Coco*'s casting of actual Latinxs to voice Latinx characters shows that it's possible to get it right—and with huge box-office returns.

Yet, the history of animation (past and present) demonstrates how creators continue to want to fix us to a limited set of cultural ingredients: food, cars, bad hombres, mysticism, and hypersexiness. In *Rango* (2011) Gore Verbinski gives audiences a Latino character, but in the form of the mystical, shaman-like nine-banded armadillo, Road Kill (voiced by Spanish-born British actor Alfred Molina). He serves the function of enlightening Rango (Johnny Depp): "Enlightenment. We are nothing without it."

The character Manny in *Cloudy with a Chance of Meatballs 2* (2013) exists in a story that's all about *food*—and its dangers. Manny licks his chops when he sees a marauding TACO-dile Supreme approach the team (accompanied by mariachi music). In *Turbo* we have hip-hop-listening Tito (Miguel Peña), who co-owns a taqueria with his brother Angelo (Luis Guzman), as well as the mechanic Paz (Michelle Rodriguez), with a rather bulbous derrière that Pixar's camera lens likes to hover over.

In *Oliver & Company* (1988) Cheech Marín plays the voice of the heavily East-LA Spanish-accented Chihuahua Ignacio Alonzo Julio Frederico de Tito (known simply as Tito). And Cheech also plays the voice of the anthropomorphic '59 Impala lowrider, Ramone, in *Cars* (2006) and *Cars 2* (2011). His license plate: "LoWNSLo." (Notably, too, Cheech and other Latino actors like John Leguizamo have voiced secondary characters in *Dora the Explorer*, including "A Crown for King Bobo" and "Captain Pirate Piggy" respectively.)

Bill: Well, *"actors gots to work, no?"* I always think about the conundrum as I watch Latinx actor after Latinx actor play Narco #1 or Hot Mama #29 or Mexican Bandit #2,345—first we have the parched, parching desert of limited roles: "how else are actors supposed to make a living" . . . and then the other barren desert of the imagination with banal, predictable roles that are so typical and stifling!

Fede: I'm of two minds when it comes to *The Simpsons* (1989–). It remains for me one of the wittiest shows on TV. Yet, while hugely popular among Latinxs, the show doesn't feature any continuously present Latino characters.

Bill: Nor does it have to—the show is a bizarro-world antidote to 1950s/'60s-era offerings like *My Three Sons* (1960–1972). That I know of, we were not on that show either. I am struggling to remember whether a Latino character ever graced the stages of *Happy Days,* but I am drawing a blank.

Fede: Only if we consider the osmosis effect: greaser brownness seeping into whiteness to make the Fonz into utter coolness. *Happy Days* is like *Archie* comics—totally devoid of color. However, let's not forget that it was Dan DeCarlo's visual skills that shaped the *Archie* comics look that inspired Jaime Hernandez to create his earth-shattering *Love & Rockets,* chock-full of Latinx characters. This said, it's hard to imagine what kind of Latinx imagination can turn today's Brownfaced comics and cartoons into something new. I'm thinking of Homer's boogie down to an identifiable Latino Mambo or Salsa tune. And at one point, Tito Puente is temporarily hired to be the music teacher at Springfield Elementary—and is also a suspect in the shooting of Mr. Burns.

The lyrics for his song, "Señor Burns" are as follows: "It may not surprise you / But all of us despise you / Please die, and fry, in Hell / You rotten rich old wretch. / Adios Viejo!" And, to smooth things over after he'd exploited Bart and Lisa at Kamp Krusty, Krusty the Klown takes them to "The Happiest

Place on Earth"—not Disneyland, but Tijuana. This episode ends with a faux montage of Bart, Lisa, and other Springfield kids wearing sombreros and getting wasted.

Bill: It's a striking montage—the first episode of season 4, "Kamp Krusty," directed by Mark Kirkland and written by David M. Stern, tosses up a classic hodgepodge of dodgy bordertown imagery.

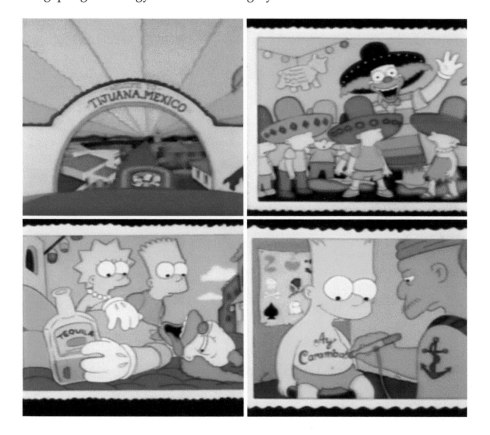

But there is no irony here as there is with Welles and *Touch of Evil*, where you are meant to be lost between the dividing line between the US and Mexico.

Here, it is clear, that Krusty, with sombrero, witnessing cock-fighting, passed out on tequila, and leading tattoo-parlor fieldtrips for Springfield's finest, is criminal, and that TJ, currently enjoying a cultural renaissance (owing to the LOSS of Gringo tourists), appears in glorious Technicolor as a den of iniquity akin to the land Pinocchio is led to by the crafty fox in Disney's classic re-imagineering of that uncanny narrative.

Fede: The creators of *The Simpsons* did include several episodes that allude to Latino-ness, but they are one-hit wonders. I'm thinking of the episode "Special Edna" that features the character Julio Estudiante working with inner-city youth. In typical *Simpsons* fashion it's a parodic palimpsest of Olmos as Jaime Escalante in *Stand and Deliver* (1988). And there was the appearance of Bumblebee Guy, the star of the Spanish-language TV network Ocho.

In a double parody both of our tradition of luchadores never taking off their mask and the slapstick of Chespirito and his show *El Chapulín Colorado,* Bumblebee Guy never takes off his costume in public, speaks in truncated and exaggerated Spanish, and confesses that he's actually Belgian.

Bill: That's *The Simpsons* at its best—parody in the best form, not totally reinforcing highly charged stereotypes but shifting them, altering them, playing with them, which is the essence of comedy.

Fede: And then Lalo Alcaraz jumped on the creative writing crew for the short-lived *Bordertown* (2016).

Bill: Yes, along with Gustavo Arellano, my SoCal partner in crime!

And for a moment there, one imagined everything was right with the world—that Lalo and Gustavo would take over the writers' room and school those hipsters Seth McFarland hired, *esos gabachos y gabachas,* about what is comedy on the verge, on the border.

And some of it worked—many of the episodes are classic *comedias de la frontera / en la frontera.* But Fox didn't know how to promote the show, and often the comedy, infused with *Family Guy* (1999–) DNA, just didn't come through in the end. But I won't knock Gustavo and Lalo for trying, for working endlessly to get that baby to fly—sometimes with their *raza* fanboys and girls screaming at them for "selling out" or getting something wrong. Having flailed at the windmills of network TV, I know how hard it is to get leverage and traction, and I think their efforts (especially at diversifying the writers room—which makes academe's ivory tower look multicultural) needs to be recognized. Gustavo's epic *OC Weekly* postmortem is as moving as it is maddening:

Last Sunday saw the bittersweet culmination of a dream I dropped 15 years ago, a dream I now want more than ever before. The occasion was the season finale of *Bordertown,* a FOX cartoon that satirized life on the U.S.-Mexico border and for which I served as a consulting producer. It was a historic series, the first cartoon starring Latinxs on prime time. And the conclusion to Season 1, titled "Viva Coyote," was my first writing credit and helped me get my Writer's Guild of America (WGA), West membership—yay! But I held no viewing party, had no friends and family over to mark the achievement. It was also the series finale for *Bordertown*, as FOX had announced its cancellation two weeks earlier. We just never got the ratings or critical buzz to justify a second season for executives. And that same week, all the networks and many cable, web and streaming outlets began announcing their new shows for the fall season—and only one will focus on Latinos (a Netflix-Univisión drama about *El Chapo*—surprise, surprise). With *Bordertown*'s axing and a similar fate befalling the Eva Longoria-starring NBC laugher *Telenovela*, that leaves just one English-language, Latino-centered show—the CW's *Jane the Virgin*—on network television, one on cable (*Lopez*, George Lopez's latest roman à clef), none on Amazon Prime (*Mozart in the Jungle,* starring Gael García Bernal, doesn't really count), one on Hulu (*East Los High*), *Narcos* on Netflix . . . and that's it. This, during the supposed Golden Age of Television. In a country in which Latinos are now the largest minority. In a year in which politicians are defaming Mexicans nonstop. In an industry based in Southern California, which reverted to Mexico in 1995. As we say in Spanish—and someone get a translator for the writers' room, won't ya?—*¿que pinche chingada?*[2]

Fede: I certainly share Gustavo's pining (laced with deep frustration) over the sounding of the death knell of *Bordertown*—and lack generally of good #browntv programming. And while I'm a junkie for *Jane the Virgin,* it's hardly sophisticated #browntv. I like that Jane's the agent—and author—of her own story. I like that it stars almost all brown folks—nearly excusing flubs like casting the Italian American Justin Baldoni as the Latinx heartthrob Rafael—but it's hard to shake the overarching mood and message: that Latinxs are straight, histrionic—deceitful—caricatures.

The mainstream's stripped down our culture into one-dimensional caricatures, including those tales many of us heard as kids about *la llorona.* We were told the myth of the angry woman who hangs out by bodies of water where she drowns children so that we wouldn't jump into those canals in and around my neighborhood in the Northern California Central Valley. Pasteurized and homogenized through the mainstream imaginary, *la llorona* has become a commercial to advertise milk: "La Llorona, Got Milk?" In maybe a minute or two, the commercial features a wispy woman whose weeping stops momentarily when she opens a fridge and pulls out a carton of milk.

She's got her *pan dulce* and is clearly in need of some *leche* to wash it down. But the weeping starts again when she discovers that it's empty. Are we to assume that she's drowned her *niños* and betrayed her *raza* for a glass of milk—signifiers of homogenized pure whiteness that's ever forestalled?

Bill: Don't be scaring me with *La Llorona* —I think I heard the real one howling at me from Chacón Creek in Laredo when I was a kid and the recent cinematic version of her, *The Curse of La Llorona,* 2019, with its 30% approval rating on *Rotten Tomatoes,*[3] is no less scary, so let's stay focused on #browntv. What say we turn to one of my favorite subjects: Food!

Fede: As you and I know well, eating in Latino culture in the US has traditionally been more than just satisfying a fundamental biological need. It's a specific appointment to meet in order to confirm, in this eating together, the social liens; it re-solidifies the social glue of the family structure and institution. Within the family hierarchy the person who presides over the table (usually the father, but it can be almost anybody in his absence) is in charge of justice, fairness, and equality: whether in gratitude because of the abundance or assessing the scarcity, in either case the head of the table's function is to adjudicate and to be sure that all get their fair share of food—and to oversee the circulation of information, comments, and anecdotes. The figure presiding over the table can even regulate when and what is acceptable to speak about during eating time, what should be the right speed at which food is to be ingested, when and why one can be excused to leave from the table, and so on. And, the *sobremesa,* that is, the time spent lingering and chatting after the meal, is a specific form of continuation of the family gathering within the Latinx culture.

Bill: I always love discussions at the *sobremesa*—we even do it in our home and did it all the years the kids were growing up. But confession time: in our Nericcio household at 1609 Hendricks in Laredo, Texas, we were as *Gabacho* as kids from Poughkeepsie! We ate dinner with TV trays in front of the idiot box, laughing to the antics of Gilligan as we consumed our spaghetti, or tuna salad, or Dinty Moore beef stew, or whatever else my tired, overworked mother had the gallantry to whip up for us each day.

Fede: TV trays at my *abuelita's*—almost as heavily lathered with the sepia hue of nostalgia in my brain as *El Chapulín Colorado* and pan dulce. There's a lot of fractal doublings going on right now: two Latinx scholars enacting the

communal ritual of the *conversación de sobremesa* about #browntv's reconstruction of Latinx identities in and through all cultural phenomena, food included.

Ralph Ellison's narrator declares, "I yam what I am." We are what we eat, in life and in the #browntv imaginary. It's our daily connection to our cultural heritage—as much as language and other daily rituals. Take the Latino written, produced and partly starred in *Ugly Betty,* for instance: it is the undocumented Latinx father Ignacio Suarez (Tony Plana) who stays at home, cooks the meals, and is the primary caregiver to his two daughters. It is during the dinners that the characters share their lives (including the coming out as gay of the cousin Justin Suarez) and the father shares his wisdom. In the silver-screen imaginary there's María Ripoll's film, *Tortilla Soup* (2001), that puts food front and center to the plot. I like that it also features a Latino *papá* (and widower) who is the anchor within the domestic—and the repository of cultural tradition generally. In this case it is Martin Naranjo (Héctor Elizondo) who cooks elaborate Sunday meals for his three daughters, each struggling with life decisions (career and love life) that threaten to pull the family apart—and destroy their connection to their Latinx roots. However, while Ignacio Suarez is gentle and kind with his daughters, Martin is more of a macho, forbidding them from speaking Spanish or Spanglish at the table. Martin's a *machista* assimilationist.

We see this also in the #browntv show *Los Americans* (2011–), where Esai Morales plays the *machista* pro-assimilationist who also demands that the children speak English at the dinner table—and this, against the fierce *abuelita* (played by #browntv's fave *abuelita* actress, Lupe Ontiveros) who insists on speaking Spanish to the new-gen Latinxs—and rejects flatly other forms of assimilation like the serving of mashed potatoes with gravy and pork chops with asparagus.

Bill: The food is key, really—I remember an Anglo student at the University of Connecticut earnestly lamenting to me about how he had no culture while I, with my homemade tortillas de arena and jalapeños, beans, et cetera, was a veritable soul man of existential depth and romanticized Latinx authenticity. I stopped for a second and told him that the Styrofoam container he was carrying with his McDonald's lunch was his *comal*-cooked tortilla, that he just didn't recognized the exoticness (and the toxicity) of his complicated food culture. Not sure he liked that.

Fede: It's a fact that food is quintessential in our culture, Bill. But it's a gastronomy that's also constantly transforming—and without assimilating to the McDs or the mash with gravy. Our *compa* Gustavo Arellano is the specialist here, of course, calling attention to all variety of hybridizations like the kimchi taco and pastrami burrito.

One way or another, food remains the center of life for Latinx *familias,* and sometimes not instantiated as a sit-down meal. In a show like *Modern Family* we might say that the creators are upending the stereotype of the Latina as somehow always affiliated with the domestic. Gloria *doesn't* cook. This could be just another instance, however, of what Molina-Guzmán identifies as a "hipster racism" that winks to audiences that it *knows* the stereotype, but in the end the show continues to reproduce ideologies of white, straight, conservative privilege. In the end, as Molina-Guzmán discusses of writer/producer Dan O'Shannon's fear of losing advertisers and audiences by showing the sullying of white purity—Gloria and Jay never kiss, even—the show replicates the deep fear of *mestizaje* that still permeates the US white national psyche.

What can I say but that Gloria's nondomestic identification, then, is yet another case of one step forward and three steps back when it comes to the construction of a complex #browntv imaginary.

Bill: I can't add a word to that! You've left me speechless.

Fede: And that we're no longer even seeing the sit-down meal in reel #browntv reconstructions nor in everyday real life does say something about how capitalism is ripping to shreds our communal rituals. For economic reasons (many of us holding down multiple jobs to pay exorbitant mortgages or rents and with no fixed days for rest and long commutes) as well as other obligations it is becoming more and more impossible for Latinx families to share meals in the evenings; it's becoming more and more difficult to meet on Sundays and share food together with affection and personal news. We might hate Esai Morales's character and the plates *sans* color (white potatoes and brown gravy) in *Los Americans,* but at least there's still the ritualized breaking of bread at dinner. Food and the Latinx family as ritual that confirms family bonds—and this not just within straight *familias,* but also LGBTQ—is a thing of the past. Likely one day we'll look back at *Los Americans* and *Ugly Betty* with the same nostalgia we do with those shows you and I seem to pine over from earlier epochs of #browntv.

SECTION V

Fear, Loathing, and the Latinx Threat

Fede: Today's #browntv reality shows fan paranoia and fear of the Brown Other. The manufacture of the Latinx Threat Narrative—a destructive discourse that Leo Chavez identifies as not only being all pervasive but as underlying the widespread prejudice about Latinxs today. Chavez says it straight: "The Latino Threat Narrative is pervasive even when not explicitly mentioned. It is the cultural dark matter filling space with taken-for-granted 'truths' in debates over immigration on radio and TV talk shows, in newspaper editorials, and on Internet blogs."[1]

Bill: I remember about ten years ago, I was a regular commentator on Gustavo Arellano's KPFK commentary show based out of Los Angeles.

I was saying then that the ground was being made fertile for a period of hate. The most popular radio commentators of the time were becoming celebrities: Glenn Beck, Ann Coulter, Rush Limbaugh (already, then, a poster child for aural hate, an analog for the televisual hate Roger Ailes had masterminded for Fox News), and, of course, my favorite whipping boy at the time, I-am-married-to-a-Mexicana-so-its-ok-that-I-hate-Mexicans, #hypocrite of the millennium, Lou Dobbs. His preachings on diseased Mexicans coming over the border to infect poor, blameless gringos was epic. I remember that I was moved at the time to create one of my ridiculous #mextasy posters immortalizing this germophobic racist hatemonger (opposite).

Wikipedia's well-researched chronicle of Lou Dobbs's fall from grace in 2009 is curious and in need of review. A subsection entitled "Exit from CNN" shares how "on the November 11, 2009 edition of his nightly broadcast *Lou Dobbs Tonight*, Dobbs announced his immediate departure from CNN, end-

ing a nearly thirty-year career at the network, citing plans to 'pursue new opportunities.'"

The July 2009 controversy around Dobbs began when he was the only mainstream news anchor to give airtime to the birther conspiracy theory. Several liberal advocacy groups, including Media Matters, and the Southern Poverty Law Center criticized Dobbs for his reporting. The controversy eventually caused CNN President Jon Klein to rein Dobbs in via an internal memorandum. In September, advocates challenged Dobbs for appearing at a FAIR conference (Federation for American Immigration Reform), a leading anti-illegal immigration group. Multiple campaigns were launched, including "Drop Dobbs" (NDN, Media Matters), and "Basta Dobbs" (Presente.org).[2]

What was happening in 2009 was only a tease for Dobbs's resurrection as a mouthpiece on Fox Business Network, where his fetid brand of fresh-baked hate appears nightly to this day. In retrospect, we can see Donald Trump and his Mexican-hating spleen for what it is: a new and improved (and more popular) version of Lou Dobbs. Or better, he becomes a patchwork-quilt avatar of Latinx loathing with Trump fusing, like Frankenstein's wretch (but much less sensitive), the hate-foaming-at-the-mouth syntax of Coulter, Dobbs, Limbaugh, and now, Richard Spencer, Sean Hannity, Milo Yiannopoulos, and Steve Bannon. I've tried to immortalize this moment in a piece called "The Four New Horsemen of the Apocalypse" for my traveling Mextasy "Circus of *Desmadres*":

Fede: You capture so well the inbreeding and deep xenophobic legacies that have morphed into a Dobbs-cum-Trump-cum-Limbaugh-cum-Beck *chupacabra* that's rearing its ugly head across the nation today. With King Cheeto and his white pointy-hatted crew, daily tweets tell the nation that we and our Latinx brothers and sisters are a swarming horde taking jobs and sneaking across borders.

I usually have a majority of Anglo students when I teach my "Latinx Pop Culture" course. They think I'm making things up or just being ultra-paranoid when talking about the making of the #browntv threat narrative; the Latinx students don't need convincing. So, I include on the syllabus reality TV shows like *Border Wars* (2010–15), *Border Patrol* (2010–15), and *Homeland Security USA* (2009). In *Whiteness on the Border* Lee Bebout sums up well the whole *tamal,* observing how these kinds of shows "cast the United States and its agents as benevolent, humanitarian actors fighting smugglers and saving migrants. The result of this savior narrative is the elision of economic and governmental policies that have fostered and exacerbated immigration and placed migrants' lives in danger."[3] And, in her trademark sharp and smart analysis, Camilla Fojas identifies ABC's *Homeland Security: USA* and A&E's *Bordertown: Laredo* (2011) as extensions of the reality TV show *Cops,* but with a difference. These shows tend to reflect, she writes, "the borderland's social and political conditions premised not on racial difference but on the typology of citizen and alien."[4] In my class, I use both Bebout and Fojas to help pry open unsuspecting eyes to the reality-#browntv of it all.

Bill: {Sarcasm-alert} But Fede, *please,* how can you write such obviously misguided things!? Didn't you read David Knowles's epic review of *Bordertown: Laredo* in the show bible of tinseltown, *The Hollywood Reporter*?!

> Executive producers Al Roker (*The Show, D.E.A.*) and C. Russell Muth (*American Chopper*) have delivered a superbly edited, documentary-style portrait of an American town and the problem threatening to overwhelm it. While each episode builds dramatic tension as initial tips and drug dealing arrests inevitably lead to the promise of taking down a major cartel shipment, the personalities of the members of the narcotics team prove just as engaging. "You know what really pisses me off?" Investigator Rodriguez yells at a woman who has just been arrested for carrying 60 pounds of packaged marijuana in the trunk of her car, and whose four-year-old daughter sits in the backseat. "You have your little girl there. I don't care what happens to you, but your little girl lying there is innocent." Far from being an exploitative show that ridicules the accused, *Bordertown: Laredo* dutifully protects the identities of its suspects, and sometimes emphasizes their humanity.[5]

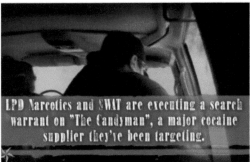

LPD Narcotics and SWAT are executing a search warrant on "The Candyman", a major cocaine supplier they've been targeting.

Seriously, this kind of paramilitary wet dream amounts to a *Central America-cization* of the US borderlands; we lived through this once before (on television for me). The episode I screened for this book with its classic anti-Mex screed is one for the books: *Bordertown: Laredo—The Candyman* (2011). IMDB's anonymous plot summary gives you the gist of the mess: "A series of controlled buys leads Roly and his C.I. [Chief Investigator] to the home of a local dealer. The SWAT team swoops in, but finds the house empty. They decide to call the bust off before suddenly spotting a car fleeing the scene. Can they nab the drug lord before his poison spills out onto the streets?"[6] Seeing the descendants of my classmates running around my hometown of Laredo on the run, gunning for lying narcos like "Candyman," is enough to make my stomach come into my mouth![7] And the notion of "poison spill[ing] out onto the streets" would make Trump, Stephen Miller, and their go-to guy on border issues, anti-Latinx Kris Kobach, go orgasmic!

Fede: No wonder the *narcotrafficante* flicks I used to pick up at the *pulga* have crossed over into the US mainstream televisual imaginary. I'm not just talking *Breaking Bad* and *Better Call Saul,* with their collapsing of the US Latinx with South-of-the-Border Américas in and through the drug trade, but the huge popularity of shows like *Narcos* (2015–), *Queen of the South* (a 2016 remake of Telemundo's super popular 2011 *La reina del sur*), and Matthew Heineman's documentary, *Cartel Land* (2015). Come to think of it, these are all on Netflix; Ted Sarandos and Reed Hastings's company seems to have a monopoly on trafficking to our living rooms the Latinx threat narrative. Of course, none of the above really get at the heart of what's happening, and here I don't mean just the BrownTelevisual construction of the threat narrative. I also mean the sensationalizing of a transamerican *narcocultura* itself—a cultural phenomenon inclusive of films, music, food, saints, fashion that has developed, as our *colega* and friend Ryan Rashotte writes, "around a billion-dollar industry that annually destroys thousands of lives while it mellows, wilts, inspires, and unhinges millions more."[8] Rashotte couldn't be more spot-on. Even a show like Fox's *Exorcist* somehow manages to slide into this narcoculture track.

Ostensibly, it's about Latinx priest Father Tomas (played by Alfonso Herrera, also appearing in *Sense8*) learning from Marcus Keane (Ben Daniels) how to fight demons. When you peel the layers back, what we see is that Tomas and Keane are traveling holy warriors ridding rural America of its demons: writ opioid addictions. It's saints, sinners, and narcoculture all packaged up as a demon-hunt adventure narrative.

Bill: A few years back I hit the streets of New York to visit NYU and deliver a talk on what I call Narcheology (or [N]archeology when I have my periodic Derrida/poststructuralism name-play withdrawals).

VISUAL NARCHEOLOGY
Scarface, Semiotics, and Spectacles of Violence in Northern Mexico and the American Southwest

I never published the presentation, but it was focused on a peculiar semiotic evolution that traced the iconography of *Scarface*, Brian de Palma's epic cinematic classic, as it made its way across the American Southwest.

What I found in Laredo, Texas, *pulgas* (swap meets; flea markets) was that images of Tony Montana (Al Pacino in Brownface?) were ubiquitous—posters, blankets, cozies, you name it, Montana and his "little friend" were plastered all over Laredo, and I suspect the savagery of that piece of cinema has a lot to do with the creative violent semiotics narcos use in dealing with their enemies.

Fede: Coyotes y pollos have likewise entered into the BrownTelevisual imaginary. Marketed as reality TV, or the real stories of coyotes (usually men) who prey upon the naive, helpless, and hopeless *imigrante* (usually women and children), we've got today the makings of what Gabriella Sanchez identifies as the "border spectacle."[9] National Geographic's series *Underworld Inc.* (2015) peddles in the business of the border spectacle. The border-patrol agent comes off as the savior once again in episodes like "Alien Stash House" and "Human Cargo"—and this sensationalized simulacra is airing on the respected National Geographic channel, not a Lou Dobbs radio *pedo*. There's never the larger picture: that women, children, and men are faced with dying of starvation in homelands, or living another day across the border. No wonder DJT has such a Build-the-Wall following.

Bill: The only places you get a better telling of the tale are in the writings of ethnographers/sojourners like Jason De León, Professor of Anthropology at UCLA. In his own words:

> I am an anthropologist whose research interests include theories of violence, materiality, death and mourning, Latin American migration, crime and forensic analyses, and archaeology of the contemporary. I direct the Undocumented Migration Project (UMP), a long-term study of clandestine border crossing that uses a combination of ethnographic, archaeological, and forensic approaches to understand this phenomenon in a variety of geographic contexts including the Sonoran Desert of Southern Arizona, Northern Mexican border towns, and the southern Mexico/Guatemala border. The UMP will be running an ethnographic/archaeological field school in the summer of 2015 in Chiapas, Mexico focused on understanding the experiences of Central American migrants crossing Mexico. I am also developing a large-scale project on urban violence, Latinos, and crime scene analysis.[10]

An "archeology of the contemporary"—I love this brave Latinx scholar's work; he actually did a forensic study of how mammalian bodies decompose (and are subjected to predators/scavengers) in the desert in order to help loved ones in Mexico and Latin America find traces of their disappeared in the no-man's-land of the American Southwest deserts. In his study, he used a pig carcass, but dressed as an actual migrant; the study was both arresting and moving. If I could subject Trump, and Bannon and Kobach, to some *Clockwork Orange*–style aversion therapy, I would force them to read De León's *The Land of Open Graves: Living and Dying on the Migrant Trail.* Jon M. Shumaker's review is worth sampling here (along with Jason's photograph[11]):

Jason de León's *The Land of Open Graves: Living and Dying on the Migrant Trail* is a disturbing book about an immense human tragedy. But somehow it's the pigs I can't get out of my head — and not just the pigs, actually, but the horrible reality of what they represent. De León buys a pig and hires someone to kill it. Shot in the head, the animal struggles mightily as the author rubs its belly, mumbling, "It's OK. It's OK." The dead pig is then dressed in underwear, jeans, T-shirt and tennis shoes and dumped beneath a mesquite. The researchers step back to record, with scientific precision, exactly what happens to it over the next two weeks.

The pig represents the body of an undocumented immigrant, de León writes, part of an experiment to understand what happens to those who die and disappear in the Sonoran Desert. He repeats this violent process four more times and writes a scientific paper about it. The conclusion is stark and inevitable: The desert eats poor people. As director of the Undocumented Migration Project, de León is conducting a long-term study using the tools and methods of anthropology to understand undocumented migration between Mexico and the U.S.

Vultures scavenge a pig carcass five days into a post-mortem decomposition experiment in the Sonoran Desert.

Courtesy Jason de León

Fede: Bill, this seems to be the kind of reconstruction—simulation—that's respectful and that works to wake people to the murderous results of the massive increase in high-tech weaponizing of the border that forces our folks to cross in increasingly deathly places. But there are those reconstructions that leave me with a gut-wrenching, retchful reaction. I'm thinking of one of the Three Amigos, Alejandro G. Iñárritu's 3D, virtual video installation piece, *Carne y Arena* (2017).

The *Associated Press* describes it thus:

You walk along a high metal fence that once divided Arizona and Mexico and into a small holding cell where you are asked to take off your shoes and socks. All around you are the abandoned shoes of migrants who have been arrested by the border patrol. When a red light flashes, you enter a large chamber with a sand floor. A ragged band of migrants crossing an expansive desert swarms around you.

For a moment, in the dusty twilight, you join their flight.[12]

And, let's not forget that shameful theme park in Hidalgo, Mexico: *Parque EcoAlberto*. With your pesos paid, you hear sirens blast as *migra* agents chase you and dogs lunge at your legs.

We're constructing this threat narrative and border spectacle ourselves, Bill. It's a modern-day version of the Beat narrative like Kerouac's *On the Road* (1957) that opened doors to Anglo America slumming it in Mexico. It's more monstrous than Gareth Edwards's Brit-flick, *Monsters* (2010), which features a white couple traversing the US–Mexico borderlands, now a quarantined area and the nesting home of Godzilla-sized aliens. Per the narrative arc, they survive the dangerous crossing of this "alien," borderland space—and experience an enlightened transcendence.

This said, there are Latinx creators who are turning tables on this Latinx threat narrative and the spectacle of the border. I'm thinking of Lalo Alcaraz's satirical cartoons—and, of course, his clear hand at play in the shaping of *Bordertown*.

Gustavo Arellano and Lalo Alcaraz sing the praises of *Bordertown* in person at a sold-out community screening at Casa Familiar's The Front Gallery, San Ysidro, California, November 13, 2015. Photo credit Carlos Solorio.

Bill: Absolutely true! Both Lalo Alcaraz and Gustavo Arellano are an avant-garde of resistance fighters using political cartoons and journalism to repopulate the national psyche with alternative snapshots of subjectivity. And unlike some of our *carnales veteranos,* they are more open to complex, gray-area manifestations of mexicanicity that are not prone to claims of essentialism. You see this in the reporting coming more and more from Latinx websites like *Mitú* and *Remezcla*—where the accent is on the diversity of Latinx subject-effects, as my *maestra* Gayatri Spivak called them back in the day.

Fede: With Robert Rodriguez's *Planet Terror* (2007) and his decolonial narratives (now deeply problematized in light of the McGowan confessions) created for his El Rey Network, we see a Latinx creator complicating further Latinx subject-effects. Put AMC's *The Walking Dead* (2010–) or SyFy's *Z Nation* (2014–) front and center in your mind, Bill. With Robert's work (and a friend of mine, his cousin Alvaro Rodriguez, as writer for El Rey), we see more clearly

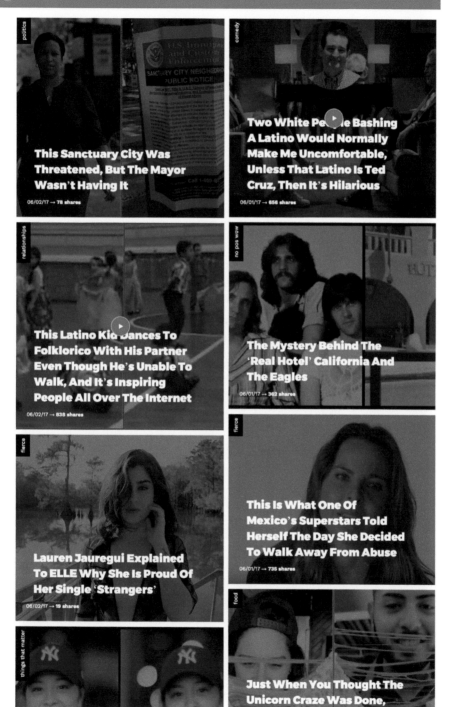

A telling montage from the *We Are Mitú* homepage (https://wearemitu.com/), June 5, 2017

how something like *Walking Dead* or *Z Nation*, which promise adrenalized chills as horror-tainment, are actually colonialist propaganda and the Latinx threat narrative all dressed up in zombie attire. In *Walking Dead*'s "Vatos" (season 1, episode 4), the Anglo savior character Rick Grimes (Brit actor Andrew Lincoln) and his multiculti ragtag team encounter some *vato locos* in a postapocalyptic Atlanta. Juan Pareja (as Morales) and Noel Gugliemi (as Felipe) exaggerate Chicanx slang and sartorial wear to be sure the audience *gets* that they are Latinx gangbangers. And, in a recent episode of *Z Nation* (season 2, episode 15), Gina Gershwin appears in Brownface as a Latina *bruja* (and leader of a pack of *calavera*-painted, machete-wielding Anglos) who imitates a stereotypical speech intonation of an East-LA *chola*. In both cases, it's the white-savior-led erasure (left behind or annihilation) of Latinxs that propels the narrative forward. If we consider our zombie-tainment options, then, Rodriguez's imaginary *is* clearing new, decolonial productive #browntv spaces.

Bill: Robert Rodriguez, Alvaro, and a guy named Robert Kurtzman (who has credits for writing on thirty episodes) have come up with a doozy of a #browntv sequel for the movie *From Dusk till Dawn* (1996), perhaps most famous for Salma Hayek's dance scene with the snakes. But it only takes a few snapshots from the series trailer to see that while the show knows its South Texas territory like the back of its hand, it is also still trafficking in a familiar line of wares: graphic violence, S&M sexuality, guns, and blood that are the trademark of Latinx semiotics according to show biz, no?

How is it different? You know that while I loves me some Robert Rodriguez, the Tejanito that could, I also think that the radically disturbing violence he spins can take a toll on the psyche (Latinx or not) and help concretize the notion of Mexicans as a synecdoche/proxy for violence that is hard to deny.

I think of this all the time when I ponder Raymond Cruz's portrayal of Tuco Salamanca on *Breaking Bad* (he returns on *Better Call Saul*). I know Raymond from way back—he played the disturbed twisted boxer Vinal in Oliver Mayer's play *Blade to the Heat* (1994) at the Mark Taper Forum in LA. He's a savvy savage actor—somewhat in the vein of Robert de Niro in his Scorsese days. As Tuco in *Breaking Bad*, he is a twisted amalgam of next-generation *narco/bandido*—he makes Gold Hat from *Treasure of the Sierra Madre* look like a quality babysitter. Tuco is mean, diseased, psychotic, and brilliant. As Cruz becomes Tuco, one is blown away by his intensity—galvanized, mesmerized, but also in shock at how a new generation of TV viewers would learn to fear Mexicans, the Spanish languages, and Latinxs in general for the ages. Netflix became Netflix through *Breaking Bad*—it's like the return to Griffith's *Birth of a Nation* where a visual racist screen drives a new medium—motion pictures.

Netflix birthed a villain more evil, drugged out, and "Mexican" than ever before.

I love this interview with Cruz that I stumbled across—as I said, he's a thoughtful *vato* and a magnificent actor, and yet, *Breaking Bad* was too much for him:

Q: How did you find out Tuco was going to die?

A: I asked them to kill me. Honestly, I wasn't looking forward to coming back and doing the part. [Laughs]. It's really difficult to pull off. They were like,

"We want you to come back and do eight more episodes." And I said, "No. I'll do one more and that's it. You guys have to kill me." They're like, "We never heard of an actor that wanted to die." And I'm like, "You don't understand. This part's really hard."[13]

And despite all the actor's mindfulness and sensitivity, I fear that Raymond Cruz's Tuco Salamanca has become *the* avatar of next-generation Latinx fear factors—the Fernando Vera character, played by Elliot Villar, from the first season of *Mr. Robot*, is not too far behind.

And the kicker to all of these is Mexican actor Manuel García-Rulfo in the second season of the Billy Bob Thornton vehicle *Goliath* (2016–), where the past star of Carl Franklin's *Bless Me, Ultima* (2013) here appears as Gabriel Ortega, a violent, narco madman who is mixed up with sexual predilections for surgical victims he has amputated! I'll say this for #browntv circa 2019—we've got range! *Puta madre, we have range!*

Fede: Is there no escape? We punch back against the #brownTV simulacra and it simply melts around our fists. I'm ready to give up, sort of. I think what we've excavated and proved here is that resistance to the Brown spectacle and simulacra is not happening with full frontal combat assaults. It's happening guerilla-warfare style, from the cover of the penumbric margins.

From those shows on El Rey, Rodriguez's films like *Machete* (2010), *Machete Kills* (2013), and *Planet Terror* (2007). Remember *Planet Terror*'s counternarrative ending when Cherry (Rose McGowan, probably around the time that Weinstein was up to no good) leads the people to the Promised Land—Tulum, Mexico— with an infant strapped to her back—a new-gen Latinx that's the product both of woman warrior Cherry and superhero badass El Wray (Freddy Rodriguez). Our colega and friend Christopher González identifies this ending as embodying the ultimate resistance with its declaration of a "post post-Latinidad" that sidesteps "overt markers of Latinidad and instead uses a handful of decisive signs of Latinidad in specific moments in his cinematic storyworlds."[14]

You're a steadfast warrior who would fight the fiercest of enemies to protect your friend and the only person I love . . . But I still hate you."

I'm waiting for Greg Berlanti and Andrew Kreisberg to make things right with their *Supergirl* (2015–) by giving some additional space (webisode or otherwise) to the Latinx character Reign (played by Samantha Arias); this would correct their "color-blind" casting of Anglo Floriana Lima (an OSU alum) as Latina lesbian detective Margarita "Maggie" Sawyer.

Bill: Fede, would you indulge me with one more trip back in the #browntv time machine? It is not so much an example of "color-blind" casting as it is "white-color" casting with a difference. It's also not something I experienced in childhood. Had I, it may have really left a scar.

It is from season 1 of *The Doris Day Show,* specifically, the third episode of the fall season entitled "The Friend," directed by Bob Sweeney and written by E. Duke Vincent and Bruce Johnson. Day, then (October 8, 1968), is at the height of her popularity—in film and, now network television, in this Arwen Productions vehicle for CBS.[15] "The Friend" is about a milk company's ad campaign that enlists Doris Martin (Day's TV character) and her gloriously beautiful (and white) children and their friends to shill their milky-white cow-gifted elixir:

Here's *tomtrekp*'s synopsis from IMDB:

> Mr. Digby has been appointed Faculty Advisor for the school's milk fund drive and has arranged for Pritchart's dairy to donate 200 pints of milk a day for the school. However, there is one condition. Pritchart wants to photograph the typical American farm family and use it in his advertising. Doris [Martin] goes along with this but Mitchell who is in charge of the shoot wants the boys to have sisters. When the boys bring home school friends to pose as their sisters it's not quite the photo Pritchart had in mind.[16]

In the episode, milk magnate Pritchart has hired an adman/photographer, Brig Mitchell, played by George Morgan, to shoot the ad. Doris Day's kids "mess up" by inviting over a friend and neighbor by the name of "Patty."

This sequence of screen grabs from my vault of Mexicans on US TV collection gives you a taste of the defining moment of the show.

"Hi Mom, I brought my sister"—says Toby Martin, Doris Martin's TV son.

Next, the photographer/adman, Mitchell, sets up the frame for the commercial:

His verdict? It's "perfect."

It's only when Patty enters the frame that the antiseptic domain of *caucasia televisualis* is endangered.

(rising string music)

Mitchell's reaction (along with the closed-captioning cue) is a priceless moment from the history of #browntv.[17]

* * *

Bill: I think this is a good place to pause and signal the beginnings of a denouement—we find ourselves with a bit of a mess, rhetorically speaking, on the cusp of a Latinx renaissance/resurgence/reappearance but simultaneously deluged by a culture industry utterly invested in outsized repetitions of the basest stereotypes.

Ultimately, we come around again to something that James Baldwin wrote that encapsulates the paradox of our #browntv universe. It is March 7, 1965, the very day Alabama State Troopers attack peaceful demonstrators crossing the Edmund Pettus Bridge, in Selma, Alabama. That very morning, Baldwin writes in the *New York Times*, in a piece entitled "The American Dream and the American Negro":

Since the moment you are born, since you don't know any better, every stick and stone and every face is white. And since you have not yet seen a mirror, you suppose that you are, too. It comes as a great shock around the age of 5, or 6, or 7, to discover that the flag to which you have pledged allegiance, along with everybody else, has not pledged allegiance to you. It comes as a great shock to discover that Gary Cooper killing off the Indians, when you were rooting for Gary Cooper, that the Indians were you. It comes as a great shock to discover that the country which is your birthplace and to which you owe your life and your identity, has not, in its whole system of reality, evolved any place for you.

In case we have not been understood, which we must, or why write: the revolution must be televised, visualized, enacted, and spread. #browntv is more than a phenomenon to be studied; rather, it is part of an evolution of a place, the birth of a revolutionary space, where an ontological incubator appears, nurturing a decidedly brown tomorrow.

The Brown Revolution
Will Be Televised

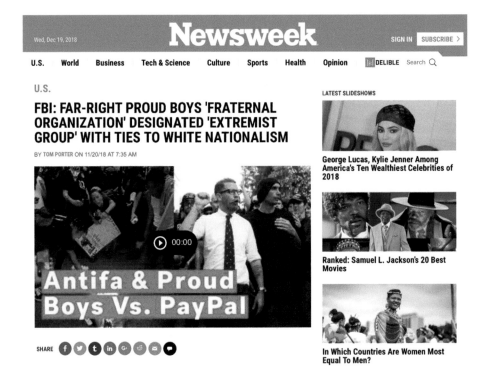

U.S.

FBI: FAR-RIGHT PROUD BOYS 'FRATERNAL ORGANIZATION' DESIGNATED 'EXTREMIST GROUP' WITH TIES TO WHITE NATIONALISM

BY TOM PORTER ON 11/20/18 AT 7:35 AM

00:00

Antifa & Proud Boys Vs. PayPal

SHARE

Fede: In the last section, we examined how the #browntv reel imaginary has consequences for the *real* lives of Latinxs. In fact, what used to be something thought of as, say, "an Arizona problem" (SB 1070) is now a national problem. Of course, it's always been a national problem. It's just that with DJT at the helm, what was more underground is now Breitbart-overground. I'm thinking of the rise of the alt-right, Fraternal Order of Alt-Knights, Proud Boys, Oath Keepers, and others with their Trump Free Speech Rallies dressed in either a fifties-styled white-boy look or sporting Spartan Warrior and Soldier for Jesus regalia. It's Walter Hill's *The Warriors* (1979) and Scorsese's *Gangs of New York* (2002), but real, not *reel*. Even the cops talk about rallies as "rumbles."

Bill: Who would have thought we would wake to this in 2017—the haunting hatred, captured by Samuel Corum in his now-signature photo for Anadolu Agency / Getty Images, will never go away.

It is as if we awake, now in our fifties, having lived through a cultural and social renaissance, born of flower power and 1960s student resistance and social justice movements, to a new now where fascism is becoming a naturalized status quo, where the enemies of progress hold the keys, and where our tomorrows are filled with fear and loathing, loathing and fear. Are we on the cusp of a new beginning, or have the contours of the carceral state, like shadows growing on a sidewalk, merely begun to engulf us in a sordid unending night—the Upside Down from *Stranger Things* as an allegory of right-wing metastasis?

Scary times for sure.

For the first time in my life I awoke in the night regretting having had a role in giving life to my children—the fear, the night-terror convulsed my consciousness—had I brought them, with and through Lila, their mother, into a world where they might suffer because of the trace of Mexico, the aroma of Latinxicity? Were they at risk—had I foolheartedly fathered unto suffering? Worst night of my life—and at 57, I have had a few!

* * *

Bill: I just finished screening Raoul Peck's *I Am Not Your Negro.* Fede, one of the most moving quotes from James Baldwin's work resounds in the film and cascaded through my mind as I reflected on our conversation here in this book, here in these pages—not for nothing has Baldwin's ghost haunted our dialogue. It is glossed in a meme I created for this book:

"There are days in this country when you wonder what your role in this country is and your place in it. How precisely are you going to reconcile yourself to your situation here and how you are going to communicate to the vast, heedless, unthinking, cruel white majority that you are here? I am terrified at the moral apathy, the death of the heart, which is happening in my country. These people deluded themselves for so long that they really don't think I'm human. I base this on their conduct, not on what they say. This means that they have become moral monsters."

Fede: If Baldwin was terrified with the "death of the heart" of the social in his day, imagine what he'd do in today's world. I think of when the Facebook group "Harvard Memes for Horny Bourgeois Teens" posted a message that likened the hanging of a Mexican child to "piñata time." These "moral monsters" got a spanking from Harvard. However, their silver spoons will surely ensure that they'll have cushy salaries and cabinet posts down the line.

Bill: We are living through the backlash (blowback?) from decades where multiculturalism was force-fed to a cowed coterie of Anglo-Americans whose hatred was kept in check by . . . decorum? Fear? Maybe even some intellectual sense that in a democracy it was better to aspire to a greater embracing of freedom and equality. And now, there is no need for that. Whatever kept hate in check, whatever kept the stereotypes virus under control, is gone.

Fede, I fear that we are living through Soderbergh's *Contagion* (2011) or Robert Wise's chilling *Andromeda Strain* (1971) but with racialized and sexualized hate strains filling in for viruses and bacteria. Or, worse, we open our eyes where Cuarón's *Children of Men* (2006) sloughs off its "science fiction" skin and emerges as a documentary—a chilling moment of Nostradamus-like prescience where the Mexican director's only error was imagining for a minute he had authored/choreographed a fiction. The real terror? *Children of Men* in the age of Trump and the alt-right is revealed as reality TV.

Fede: We had momentum gaining with Brown and Black Lives Matter along with the Occupy Movement, but where's our Brown Revolution? Have we become paralyzed by the high-wattage fear-mongering: violence against our people. Forced separation of family. Our *niños* caged like monsters. (To wake new generations of children and parents to this, I transformed the horrors of what's happening in today's borderlands into my children's book, *The Adventures of Chupacabra Charlie,* forthcoming with OSU Press in 2020.)

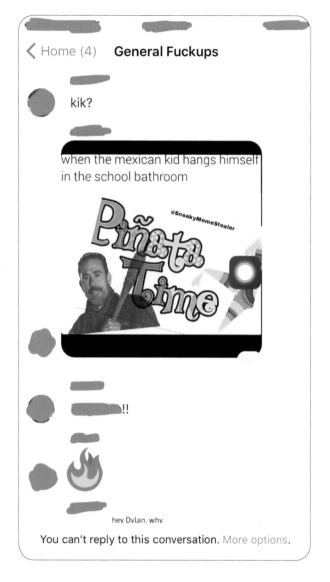

Bill: But, Fede, our revolution is not totally dead on arrival. It might actually be on the brink of revival. I'm thinking of political and cultural activists like Alexandria Ocasio-Cortez, Myriam Gurba, Sandra Valls (a fellow Laredense), Lalo Alcaraz, and Gustavo Arellano (pictured below with the late, great Anthony Bourdain). There's something amazing brewing in Latinxlandia—in the way that Lalo's deep consulting work on *Coco* (2017) smashed it into the stratosphere.

And #browntv certainly also extends now beyond television—Lalo's streaming presence as a radically progressive political cartoonist needs to be appreciated and studied more; the book by Héctor D. Fernández L'Hoeste, *Lalo Alcaraz: Political Cartooning in the Latino Community,* makes great strides in this vein.

You can sense Lalo Alcaraz's dynamic wit in one of his cartoons, below, that appeared as we were deep into this book—how it folds together, with savvy semiotic cunning, the best of #browntv. In a sense, Alcaraz's work is an example of what happens when you take influential elements from the

culture industry (DC Comics, Hollywood, *MAD Magazine,* and Walmart) and fuse them via *xicanosmosis* (the fusing of cultural elements from both sides of the US–Mexico border) with progressive, pro-immigrant, pro-America (in the best sense), social justice activism that contests the injustice (and hypocrisy) of our current political nexus. That the action goes down in the late Sam Walton's Walmart—the epitome of poor, white, working-class consumerism—makes the piece even more compelling.

Fede: Maybe I don't see the revolution because it's everywhere. Today's tech[x]-mex media and digital communication platforms allow us to expand

our Latinx multimediated guerilla-warfare and mobilization tactics. I think of the work of Librotraficante.com, originally organized by some of our beloved Latinx lit authors: Denise Chávez and Dagoberto Gilb. I think of the zines created by the St. Sucia collective whose muse is not the Virgin de Guadalupe but rather the co-created La Santa Sucia, who celebrates all things queer, corporeal, and, well, dirty. I think of the Undocuqueer movement and Julio Salgado's radical Latinx comics.

Bill: Yes, as with the vivid illustration, sampled opposite: "I am undocuqueer, because I can't be one without the other," the poster intones, Salgado's sharp lines and keen voice coming through his digital canvas with power and conviction.

Yes, and there's the crazy fiction by Salvador Plascencia (*People of Paper*) and Los Bros Hernandez (still fighting the good semiotic fight with *Love and Rockets* and their various side projects) that prove that there are mighty forces to be countenanced in digital and analog (OG!) narrative realms.

Fede: I wonder, Bill, if we can make the case for Latinx eroticism and self-created porn as yet another site of radical awakening within an otherwise homogenizing BrownTelevisual imaginary. I'm not talking *Hot Hispanics* volumes 1 through 3. No, I'm thinking radical, self-determined and Latinx agentful celebrations of the Latinx body and desire. In a piece I wrote on Gilbert Hernandez's standalones like *Birdland* (1990–91, 1994) and his neo-noir pulps, I make the case that his polymorphous perverse erotica works as a critique of capitalism and heterosexual romance. (See the introduction and the chapter "Recreative Graphic Novel Acts" in *Graphic Borders*.) Gilbert's precious, leather-bound *Garden of the Flesh* is small enough (6 × 4.75 inches and designed by "J. Feeli Pecker") to hold with one hand, nudge-nudge, wink-wink.

It's chock-full of erections, ejaculations, orgasms, and nonwhite characters—and these as the counternarrative to the Old Testament's origin stories. Recall that after the tragic loss of lives in Orlando with that queerphobic murderous rampage at the Pulse, many in the Latinx LGBTQ community celebrated erotica—a way to affirm the many ways we exist as derring-do subjects with very real bodies.

I'm also thinking of artist Alma Lopez and thinking, too, of Junot Díaz's Oscar Wao and the way the erotic entangles with Latinx masculinity. I'm thinking of the kick-ass, Latinx feminist and queer comics by Kat Fajardo, Vicko, Laura Molina, Liz Mayorga, Gabby Rivera, Dave Ortega, Ivan Velez Jr., and Serenity Serseción. Think of John Jenning's boot-stomping, Blatinx badass queer superhero drawn for the cover of my *Latinx Superheroes in Mainstream Comics*. Think of the queer *cholo* pinto art and *loteria* cards.

Bill: Yes, absolutely right—your graphic reverie brings to mind the work of Latinx artist Nanibah Chacón (who also self-identifies as Native). Chacón fuses Native and Latinx shapes and emotions in works that evoke the human form in pursuit of being, of ontological presence—the kind of ontological substance that stereotypes work to destroy. Her "Chief's Blanket," opposite, evokes this fused vein where the indigenous and the "Mexican"—already conceptual spheres suffused by the other—unfold at once onto the viewer.

Then there is Audrya Flores, an out-of-this-world artist whose paintings, installations, and concept art speak to a sexual presence not divided from the spirit/body matrix. And it is a matrix—a complex, blood- and sex-filled constellation of work that evokes a Latinx "sexy" that is more ontological than outright carnal or sexual. Here, in "Take Care" (11 × 9 inches, tissue paper, ink, pins, mescal beans in shadowbox, 2015), Flores says the emphasis is on "relationships," but we know from a careful scrutiny of the work that the artist cares as well about the body, the disembodied spirit and more. The pinned paper cut-out figures are truncated, decapitated, and yet united—their tattooed same-sex forms framed by a fundament of red cactus fruits that underscore a fecundity that the chopped bodies would seem to counterpoint.

And with "Reanimate," Flores is also telling a story of being, of ontology, the masked female form evokes the phoenix (and Shelley's *Frankenstein* via the title)—wretches returning to demand their moment in the limelight, on the level of sentience, subjectivity, and being. But this "wretch" is also beautiful, a chimera of parrot, white being, and brown being, stitched together

in a bestial panoply both lovely and uncannily disturbing.[1] Flores, however, maintains a problematic identity, an obscured *cara* (or displaced, if you wish, by the parrots).

Last, there's the work of a local San Diego artist, Eddy Rose. Her piece "The Power of the Concha" plays on the semiotic sisterhood of the Concha (shell) and the pussy, the shell, since (at least) Botticelli's "Birth of Venus" connected to the idea and figure of female sexuality—but Rose's is also "having a laugh" and punning, as "pussy power" and Western Art History dance a duet on her

canvas. With "Salt & Grease in between the Sheets," Rose evokes the carnal/culinary dimensions of Latinx sexuality—a sexuality at home with sensual representations of female desire and open to the kinky offerings of alternative sexualities (and junk food, as McDonald's fries censor one breast, while the greasy pizza slice does nothing to obscure Rose's female nude).

Oddly enough, all these artists got fed to my *ojos* through the latest conduit (electronic syringe) for #browntv, Instagram—what McLuhan would make of this still-evolving medium keeps me up at night. But I digress. . . .

The question remains can these far-from-the-mainstream artists, Fede, compete with a mass culture filled with traditional, stereotyped erotica? A mass-media cauldron literally teaming with "Hot Latina Girls . . . Sexy Hispanic

Women—Legs, Boobs, & Ass Pics"—the worlds of Pornhub where objectified Latinas are the rule?[2]

Fede: It's not that they compete, Bill; they offer powerful toeholds of resistance. We can lodge our bodies and minds into these resistant Latinx erotic spaces and together make revolution.

We're also subverting from within, Bill. I'm also thinking about how the Latinx silver-screen erotica has been used within the mainstream to disrupt the spectacle making of #browntv. There's that carefully composed shot in the opening sequence of *Machete* where Rodriguez's camera eye pauses over an Adelita calendar then cuts to a badass and totally nude "Chica" character (Mayra Leal) kicking some *culo,* including Machete's (Danny Trejo). Or, in *Machete Kills,* Rodriguez gives Latinx Sofía Vergara (as Madame Desdemona) a slammin' machine-gun bustier. The Latinx erotica is blasting holes through a long history of the mainstream's control over our body electric.

Bill: True, but you have to balance that with all the delirious, dumb, objectified *"Mami Chulas"* that besmear the interwebs and the synapses of its mesmerized consumers. Take for instance the increasingly popular line of Border Patrol pornography all the rage on Pornhub—we will spare our readers the panoply of images and share a "chaste" screengrab of a google search:

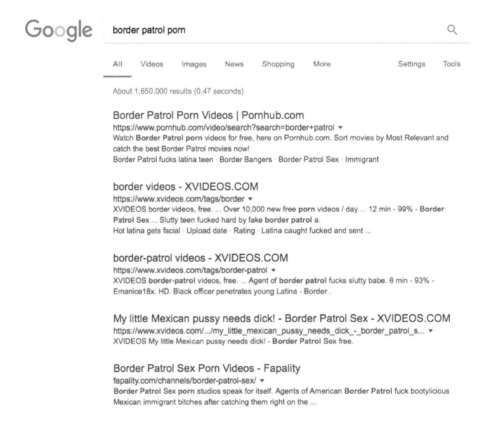

Fede: Do we take offense or celebrate Latinx porn, Bill?

Bill: Like everything else, it depends—Gilbert Hernandez's *Birdland* is one thing; Pornhub's Border Patrol rape porn is something altogether else!

Fede: What is Latinx porn, anyway? I mean, you can watch on your smartphone naked, copulating brown bodies in daylight riding the bus to work.

It's a topic tossed around by some serious intellectuals. It's made by serious Latinx creators. Certainly, there's a Latinx pop cultural phenomenon that does the trick of stimulating the imagination for an ejaculate means to an end.

Yet, what was considered pornographic a decade ago might not be today. Put otherwise, do we think of Latinx erotica and porn only as masturbatory stimulus? Are Latinx creators using lensing and editing (and all variety of other shaping devices) to create a reverse scopophilia that articulates a brown woman's desire and a brown queer gaze?

Bill: Of course, there is more there—and that's the problem with drawing too many conclusions based on generalizations. While not porn, consider the erotic threesome that brings Cuarón's *Y Tu Mamá Tambien* (2001) to its, pardon the pun, climax.

Ana Morelos (Ana López Mercado), Tenoch Iturbide (Diego Luna), and Julio Zapata (Gael García Bernal) give themselves over to a cacophony of hedonistic three-way pleasure that provides some sensual distraction and respite from the cancer destroying Ana's body and soul, and the unspeakable desire (between Tenoch and Julio). Here the sex is hot and visceral, if not pornographic, and yet in the hands of cinematographer Emmanuel Lubezki and director Cuarón, the action is used to chronicle a breakdown in the relationship, fueled by class difference and biases (not to mention the naturalized pejorative of being indigenous/"*naco*"), which is the reel/real purpose of the film. I love this about this film—it is "hot" in the classic, base sense of spurring a sensual reaction in its viewers, but it is also hot intellectually in that it forces you to think another way or to witness the limits for change when it comes to sexuality, desire, and the Latinx *dasein*.

Fede: Cuarón's slow-gazing Latinx erotic optic enraptured even the most machista of compadres, Bill. He's got a gift for interweaving the sensual pleasures of polymorphous perverse bodies with the political. *Children of Men* takes us somewhere similar, and different. When you visited The Ohio State University in the fall of 2017 you lectured on *Children* and ejaculate.[3]

Bill: Yes, I was spinning once again my favorite tale from the Old Testament regarding the only man more miserable than Job from the Book of Job: Onan. Onan, who made the mistake of spilling his seed (without procreating), is, of course, destroyed by an Old Testament angry white God/Man who will not have sex perpetrated without "issue," without conception, without breeding. It is a moment of animal husbandry that won't get topped till that short *vato* with the strange mustache takes Lindbergh and crew's rancid ideas regarding eugenics and attempts to create the "master race." My point in the lecture was to examine Cuarón's (again!) focus in *Children of Men* on procreation and migrations. I imagine I wanted to scandalize your undergraduates with lurid allusions to gods destroying men for masturbating (spilling seed), but what I really wanted to underscore was Cuarón's prescient understanding about the connection between sex, pleasure, class, migration, and the carceral state—Huxley's *Brave New World* is actually quite similar.

Fede: Let me wrangle us back to TV, the true north of our tête-à-tête, by recalling here Molina-Guzmán's concept of "hipster porn." She uses this to identify, in so many words, the making of a #browntv that at once winks at the stereotypes and continues to reproduce them. Well, it's doubly so when it comes to Latinx LGBTQ subjects, Bill. I'd like to introduce a term that might capture well this neoliberal winking: hipster intersectionalism. Afrolatino (Cuban-

heritaged) Oscar Nuñez in *The Office* is a case in point. Steve Carell's performing of Michael as an inept boss excuses his (and the straight white hip audience watching the show) Latinx-queer-bashing. There's that moment when
Michael tells Oscar he's going to have a colonoscopy and asks: "In your experience, what should I be expecting, in terms of sensation. Or, emotions. [pause]
Is there anything I can do to make it more pleasurable for me or for Dr. Shan-
dri? My main concern is should I have a safe word?" And then there's that
moment when Michael asks Oscar, "Is there a term besides Mexican that you
prefer? Something less offensive?" Like so many others, Oscar was a missed
opportunity. For the only Latinx gay character on prime-time TV—actually,
the only queer of color on prime time—the show writers seriously screwed up.
I'm not even going to go into the characterization of Oscar as the prissy, smug
gay Latinx character—the only way straight writers of TV can imagine queer-
ness: from straight Eric McCormack's performing of a straight guy's idea of
the gay character Will Truman (*Will & Grace*) to *Star Trek: Discovery*'s Anthony
Rapp's performance as the uptight Science Officer, Paul Stamets.

Bill: Well there's nothing surprising there, Fede! Just as we should not look
to Hollywood for progressive, generative ethnographies, we should not look
to television or corporate-controlled, streaming internet-based fountains of
entertainment for insight into the queer *dasein*—or straight ones for that matter. *The Office*, like *Seinfeld*, offers signature moments in the history of television, and yet, for all their success in breaking the mold, and "making history,"
they also, in the end, reinforce particular histories, particular stories that then
get retold again and again and again.

Fede: And yet we might have some silver linings snaking through the dark cumulonimbus clouds of televisualandia, Bill. There's Selena Gomez's production of Netflix's *13 Reasons Why* (2017), where the writers create a fully fleshed-out Latinx gay character, Tony Padilla (Christian Navarro), with substantive screen time that reveals his complex struggle at home (a *machista papá* and Catholicism) and with his white boyfriend. He also reinserts complex agency and complexity into a long history of the Latinx greaser stereotype—the slick-haired sociopath we mentioned earlier with *la familia Grandi* in *Touch of Evil.* Tony drives a '68 Ford Mustang, sports a '50s leather jacket, and is coifed like the best of our zoot-suiter ancestors. But he brings a radical *queering* to all of this. And, as the keeper of the secrets (the confessional tapes), he's the subject that actually controls the flow and outcome of the plot.

I'm also thinking of Mexico-born Argentinian/Honduran Latinx lesbian actor Roberta Colindrez (known for her role as Joan in the Broadway adaptation of Alison Bechdel's *Fun Home*), who plays a genderqueer Mexican American in Amazon Prime's *I Love Dick* (2017). Her character Devon's more than a sidebar to the show. She's likely the most powerful queer Latinx subject (actor/role) to appear on TV ever. In one of many powerful scenes, she commands her (their) partner to "suck my cock."

Bill: She's a savvy Latinx force in streaming television, to be sure. In an interview for *Vanity Fair,* Colindrez shares that "it's time that we allow ourselves to be monsters," going on to add how she loves "seeing Roberta explore a queer cowboy masculinity that exist[s] alongside Dick's heteronormative machismo strut."[4]

Fede: I'd like to end this rollercoaster ride through the #browntv imaginary by at once celebrating the Latinx active transformation of mainstream pop culture—and by reminding us that we need to keep vigilant and have all our senses and brain processes attuned to how #browntv with its reconstructed *reel* Latinxs continues to warp in sadistic and tragic ways the real lives of Latinxs in the US.

Indeed, until we truly live in a postrace, postfeminist, postclass, post-everything world, then our #browntv intersectional optic will be necessary. It'll be necessary to identify our transformative achievements. It will be necessary to call out the massive overrepresentation of white, straight men behind and in front of televisual lenses that continue to willfully erase Latinx subjects and experiences.

Bill: And to yours, I add my concluding thoughts. They take me back to a simulacra Chicano, Freddie Prinze, prowling national TV back in the day

Tempo/TV-Radio

Ethnic dispute brews over Prinze's 'Chico'

"He's so good he's frightening. At the age of 20 his professionalism is simply incredible. Freddie is the type of performer who emerges once every 10 years."—A seasoned Hollywood observer.

"Freddie isn't behaving like a Chicano. He is too caught up in the star thing. One time I offered to take him to El Barrio, but he has no time for that. He is too busy guesting on the Johnny Carson Show!"—Ray Andrade, associate producer of Chico and the Man.

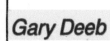 Gary Deeb

TELEVISION'S HOTTEST new star is an innocent bystander who has become the unwilling storm-center of a sociopolitical controversy that threatens the health of TV's most popular new program.

Freddie Prinze, the 20-year-old standup comic-turned-actor, is unquestionably a splendid performer and an ingratiating personality. Beset with mediocre scripts and a studio audience that sounds like it's been shooting speed, he and veteran Jack Albertson still have managed to boost Chico and the Man to spectacular popularity and critical success.

But all is not rosy in the day-to-day world of Freddie Prinze.

Prinze, you see, is an American of Puerto Rican and Hungarian descent. The character he plays in Chico and the Man is a Mexican-American. The popular term is Chicano.

AND THERE ARE those who say it's just not right for a Puerto Rican kid from New York to play a Chicano youth from Los Angeles. About a half-dozen Chicanos are constantly picketing NBC's Burbank studios, and associate producer Andrade, who was hired basically to appease L. A.'s Chicano community, is on their side.

"The way Prinze is doing the role is part Jewish and part Italian," says Andrade. "He must become more Chicano. A Puerto Rican just doesn't bring authenticity to the show."

Andrade is the former president of Justicia, a Mexican-American social action federation. And not only is he turned off by Prinze getting the title role, he also believes the program itself is offensive to Chicanos.

"I think the character of Chico is cheap and demeaning," he declares. "The old man at one point tells the kid to get out of the garage—'and take your flies with you.' Chicanos don't like that line."

THERE'S AN ALARMING poverty of social consciousness in Andrade's statement. Albertson's character is a crusty old WASP, a bigot from the word go, who slurs Chico's ethnic background with no regard for the young man's feelings.

Like it or not, such louts do exist. They number in the millions. And all of Andrade's bellyaching will not change that indisputable fact.

If TV comedy programs are to be prohibited from reflecting certain ugly realities of contemporary American life, then I guess we'll have to settle for the "relevance" of Ozzie & Harriet, Leave It to Beaver, and Me and the Chimp.

AS FOR Andrade's beef about a Puerto Rican playing a Chicano, again I'm aghast. I don't know many Mexican-Americans, so it's hard for me to comment on the charge that Prinze is blowing the ethnic aspects of Chico.

But to automatically rule out an actor from portraying a person of a different heritage, as it seems Andrade would like to do, is an exasperatingly moronic standard.

Jack Albertson isn't Irish but his performance in "The Subject Was Roses" was superb. James Caan, a Jew, was entirely believable as Sonny Corleone in "The Godfather." Danny Thomas, who's Lebanese, played a Jew in the remake of "The Jazz Singer" and was quite good. And Ernest Borgnine was magnificent as the dumpy Italian butcher in "Marty."

And on and on. Freddie Prinze is a charming, talented young man who was ready for success. He is one of the joys of the new fall TV season.

He doesn't deserve the grief he's getting. Especially not from a featherbedder like Ray Andrade.

with *Chico and the Man.* Gary Deeb, entertainment columnist for the *Chicago Tribune,* writes how Prinze overcame poorly written scripts, powering *Chico and the Man* to great success. He adds to this how Prinze is of Puerto Rican and Hungarian descent, yet plays a Chicano character. The popular term is *Chicano,* fanning controversy and leading to protests by the LA Chicano community. Deeb remarks, too, on how bigots like Albertson's character exist and that any "bellyaching" won't change this. He goes on to write, "If TV comedy programs are to be prohibited from reflecting certain ugly realities of contemporary American life, then I guess we'll have to settle for the 'relevance' of *Ozzie & Harriet, Leave It to Beaver,* and *Me and the Chimp.*"[5]

When I first read this, the line that kept *ringing in my eyes* (!?) more than any other line by Deeb was: "Like it or not, such louts do exist. They number in the millions. And all of Andrade's bellyaching will not change that indisputable fact."

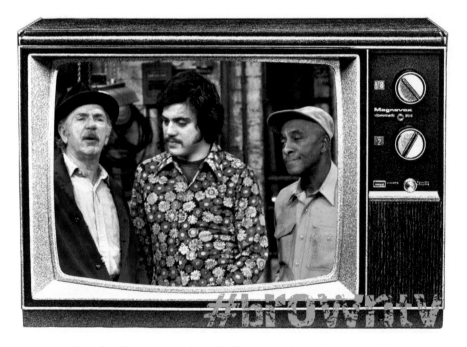

"Into the #browntv Realm," Guillermo Nericcio García (2016)

"They number in the millions"—again Andrade's lucid words return to me, ringing in my ears and scorching my eyes; Andrade's conclusion regarding the racist audience of the soon-to-be-very-troubled Prinze (he suicides in January 1977) is bracing. As he's right—and they are out there now with their tiki torches and their Nazi-youth pallor.

And the next thing out of Deeb's (dweeb's?) mouth, suggesting that Andrade's asks that the Puerto Rican star hang out in "El Barrio," is *bellyaching*.

Reasonable readers can infer Gary Deeb's point: What's with all the nuance? What's the difference between Puerto Rican and Chicano? What's all the fuss? And Deeb even cops to the fact that Chicago-based television reporters are not hanging out in the Pilsen district—which was, at the time, growing more and more Mexicano:

> The Czechs had replaced the Germans, who had settled there first with the Irish in the mid-19th century. Although there was an increasing Mexican American presence in the late 1950s, it was not until 1962–63 when there was a great spurt in the numbers of Mexican Americans in Pilsen due to the destruction of the neighborhood west of Halsted between Roosevelt and Taylor Streets to create room for the construction of the University of Illinois at Chicago. Although this area was predominantly Italian American, it was also an important entry point for Mexican immigrants for several decades. Latinos became the majority in 1970 when they surpassed the Slavic population.[6]

And we have not come far at all in our forty-three years since this column fragment appeared—a brief, inconsequential chapter in the history of #browntv. But maybe for us and for our readers, a cautionary tale, an allegory to cap off our conversation, with the revelation that our work is far from over. Deeb's assured declarations regarding the insanity of the criticisms of Prinze reveal the blinders we now associate with white privilege—the blindfolds that render sensitivity to the play of ethnic bodies nonexistent.

Fede: You've inadvertently brought a Latinx elephant into the room, Bill, so we must further prolong our tête-à-tête. What do we do with Louis C.K.? First, there's his *passing* as a ginger-haired, accentless, light-skinned Latinx. Yet, he's never denied being Latinx, being Mexican. And, he's very cognizant that his skin color has afforded him a pass in ways that, say, it hasn't for George Lopez.

Second, there's his recently revealed compulsive masturbating that, because of his power as one of the most famous comedians, led to a history of sexual abuse and violation of women (comedy duo Dana Min Goodman and Julia Wolov as well as Abby Schachner, Rebecca Correy, and others).

Let me begin with bringing up his fraught relationship to his Mexicanness; that is, his twisted relationship with his Mexican *papá*. We know from his biography that he was estranged from his *papá*. And, we see this turned into #browntv in the episode "Dad" (season 3, episode 8, August 16, 2012),

which features his aborted attempt to see his father. The scene unfolds as follows: he's on his way to see his father in Boston, but on the way, he vomits
and develops a rash from anxiety; he also hears voices: the rental-car GPS
asks him: "Why are you being such a little pussy about this?" Then it states:
"He's your father. It's not like he touched your dick or something." Once he
arrives outside the house where he's supposed to meet his father, Louis runs
away, jumps on a three-wheeler motorbike, motors to Boston harbor, gets on a
speedboat and leaves. Safely away from the *papá,* he laughs, smiles, then looks
once again troubled and sorrowful. He has a visceral reaction to his Mexican
papá. He's never seen him, but he's there like the scariest of *chupacabras.*

Can we put Louis on the Latinx couch? I mean the guy grew up with three
sisters and was raised by a single mom (an OSU alum). What made him a
misogynist? Was it the monstrous father? Catholicism? In interviews Louis
talks about getting into drugs as a teen, then later becoming addicted to porn
on the internet as well as about how post-fame sex became a way for him to
self-medicate and assuage deep anxieties. Is there something to this?

Bill: Nathan Rabin, on *The Onion's AV Club,* ventured much of the same,
regarding this contested, Oedipus-stained celebrity (did he, too, masturbate,
but this time, in front of Louis C.K.?). For Rabin, the "Dad" episode is a "mind-
fuck"[7] He asks: "Why is Louie's creepily continental uncle played by the same
actor (an Academy Award winner no less) who played an unrelated voyeur
in *Louie's* second season? Why does the prospect of seeing his father make
Louie physically ill? What has Louie's father done to him?" And, Rabin con-

cludes, the episode "doesn't just leave us with more questions than answers: it leaves us with nothing but questions."[8]

It's complex—the man's name is Louis C.K., but the show is called *Louie*—and his real, given name is Louis A. Székely—he's the son of Mary Louise Davis and Luis Székely, an economist—Luis being "the son of Dr. Géza Székely Schweiger, [who] was a Hungarian Jewish surgeon whose family moved to Mexico, where he met C.K.'s paternal grandmother, Rosario Sánchez Morales."[9]

Since the scandal broke, he's become a monstrous masturbating enigma and, apparently, a devoted, thoughtful father. He's a raging, self-loathing "Mexican" laughing at his father's uncircumcised penis in his stand-up comedy routines, and a thoughtful filmmaker problematizing the relationship between father and son with nuance on a television show. The consequences of being Mexican, of living as a Latinx celebrity who can pass for a *ginger* 'Merican in the flow of the American mainstream, also makes us recognize how necessary it is for us to look closely at his oeuvre—in the short term everything will be read in the shadow of his spectacular onanism (itself a sin of course in a neo-Puritan America that seeks to punish pleasures of all stripes).

The actual facts of the event need some record, and luckily, the ace scribes at *New York* magazine and their online incarnation, the *Vulture*, produced one—that also records Louis C.K.'s statement after the events surfaced publicly:

November 9, 2017

The *Times* publishes its story, in which five separate women came forward to accuse C.K. of proposing to or actually masturbating in front of them in professional settings. Comedy duo Dana Min Goodman and Julia Wolov say the comedian masturbated in front of them in a hotel room at the 2002 U.S. Comedy Arts Festival in Aspen, an account that matches up with the Gawker blind item. Afterward, Goodman and Wolov say that C.K.'s manager Dave Becky told them to stop telling the story of the incident. The following year, comedian Abby Schachner claims C.K. began masturbating and describing his sexual fantasies when she called to invite him to one of her shows. Another performer, Rebecca Corry, says C.K. asked her if he could masturbate in front of her while they worked on a pilot together in 2005. (She says she declined; the pilot's producers Courteney Cox and David Arquette both confirmed Corry spoke to them about C.K.'s behavior.) The fifth woman, who has chosen to stay anonymous, says C.K. repeatedly would masturbate in front of her in the offices of *The Chris Rock Show,* where they both worked.

After one of the incidents, C.K. allegedly attempted to apologize and explain his behavior. In a Facebook message to Schachner, he wrote "Last time I talked to you ended in a sordid fashion. That was a bad time in my life and I'm sorry." (The apology took place in August 2009, three days before FX announced it would make *Louie*.)

Hours before the story is published, the distributor of *I Love You, Daddy* cancels the film's New York premiere. C.K.'s scheduled appearance on Stephen Colbert's show is also canceled.

November 10, 2017

In a statement, Louis C.K. confirms that the stories in the *Times* report are true. "At the time, I said to myself that what I did was okay because I never showed a woman my dick without asking first, which is also true," C.K. says. "But what I learned later in life, too late, is that when you have power over another person, asking them to look at your dick isn't a question, it's a predicament for them. The power I had over these women is that they admired me. And I wielded that power irresponsibly."[10]

In a sense, it is madness—here we have a kind of subterranean Mexican, not even a Chicano, as he was born and raised in Mexico till he was seven or eight—a Mexican whose mother tongue is Spanish. After a career of failures and humble success, he finally hits the big time, his #browntv show, *Louie*, a blockbuster hit and critically acclaimed (the whispers are that Louis C.K. is the next "Woody Allen"; we just did not know then in what way!). It's awful because, in a way, his self-pleasuring, with unwilling audiences, apes a pattern of sexual untowardness always already associated with Latinx folks.

Fede: At least in terms of father figures (*machistas*), can we draw some parallels to Richard Rodriguez? In *Days of Obligation: An Argument with My Father* (1992), he first codes the father as the space of Mexico, as *macho,* active, and hard, versus the *indio* of his mother, who is coded as passive, and soft. Then he undergoes a deep transformation (from his assimilationist self in *Hunger of Memory*) once he actually travels to the space of the father—to Mexico:

I am on my knees, my mouth over the mouth of the toilet, waiting to heave. It comes up with a bark. All the badly pronounced Spanish words I have forced myself to sound during the day, bits and pieces of Mexico spew from my mouth, warm, half-understood, nostalgic reds and greens dangle from long strands of saliva.[11]

And, as *Days of Obligation* draws to an end, Rodriguez seems to learn to celebrate such "impure" spaces as Tijuana not as a chaotic dystopia that threatens to swallow his identity but rather as a city that exists in a fully miscegenational present—a space that is already "here."[12] Perhaps this is the step Louis C.K. never managed to take?

Bill: He's thoughtful and less of a self-loathing hypocrite than Richard Rodriguez was back in the day—maybe we give him some time. Or not. That is up to the reader, the viewers of #browntv.

Fede: Yes, much work still needs to be done, and not just in the world of scholarship and cultural production. For every *True Blood* or *Brujos* there's still a dozen more shows like *The Walking Dead* or *Drink, Slay, Love* that flatten us—even as vampires or *brujos* or zombies.

Much work has to be done at the level of politics, policy and law making, education, and within deep socioeconomic structures. Without systemic change, Latinxs will continue to be tragically underrepresented in college; they will continue to be cornered in ways that disallow the full realization of their creative and intellectual potentialities. And the abundance of Latinx presence in pop culture today is relative.

I'm going to trot out the stats once again, Bill. As we already mentioned in the beginning of our #browntv odyssey, we Latinxs make up 18 percent of the population, yet we exist in less than 2 percent of mainstream cultural phenomenon. And, as we've examined herein, plenty of that 2 percent is actively denigrative: from social media platforms like the above-mentioned Harvard Facebook group, with its abhorrent analogy of the lynching of Latinx *niños* to *piñatas,* to the malapropistic, hypersexualized Sofía Vergara as Gloria in *Modern Family.*

We are living an incredible moment in the history of #browntv and Latino/a pop *cultura* generally. We are also feeling more intense anxiety about what such an *arrival* means in terms also of our *erasure.*

Bill: If the history of television has taught us anything—and this is as true of #browntv as anything else—we best stay tuned. For now, I am going to turn off the TV and read a good book.

NOTES

Notes to Introduction

1. Wikipedia, "Cristela."

Notes to Section I

1. Valdes, "Is Porn That Depicts the Subjugation of Hispanic Women Tied to the Rise of Hate Crimes Against Latinos?"
2. Wikipedia, "Lynda Carter."
3. My only proof for this is me and my sister Josie laughing our asses off at Mel Blanc's cunning "Mexicanesque" ministrations.
4. Begley, "Sofia Vergara Was Literally Put on a Pedestal in a Completely Sexist Bit at the Emmys."
5. Federal Communications Commission, *Hispanic Television Study.*
6. See, for instance, Uffalussy, "Why Are Latino Viewers the Most Important for Networks?"
7. Molina-Guzmán, *Latinas and Latinos on TV,* 9.
8. Peretz, "Rose McGowan."
9. *Sanford and Son* (season 2, episode 8) "The Puerto Ricans Are Coming!" (aired November 10, 1972, on NBC).
10. "Coco."
11. Bradshaw, "Texas Roadhouse Employee."
12. "The Man Who Is Manolito!"

Notes to Section II

1. Laredo, Texas, did not have a broadcasting local ABC affiliate station until I was fourteen or so in 1975—and we didn't have cable television at our house until I

was sixteen or so. So it is that my nostalgia for television in/on the border is the memory of analog, tube-television and rabbit-ear antennas, a mishmash of major US network affiliates in Laredo, and Mexican stations from Nuevo Laredo, Texas, next door.

2. Egner, "'Ozark' on Netflix."

3. Wikipedia, in this regard, is clear! "Lou Diamond Phillips was born at the Subic Bay Naval Station in the Philippines, the son of Lucita Umayam Arañas and Gerald Amon Upchurch, a crew chief on a C-130 in the United States Marine Corps. His father was an American of Scottish-Irish and one-quarter Cherokee descent, and his mother, a native of Candelaria, Zambales, is Filipina, with distant Chinese, Japanese, Hawaiian, and Spanish ancestry" (Wikipedia, "Lou Diamond Phillips").

4. For a great review of Phillips as manufactured Latino, see Vargas, "5 Movie Roles That Made Lou Diamond Phillips an Honorary Latino."

5. See Nericcio, "Now You Can Insert 'Maria, the Maid' into Any Project You Dream Up!!!!." A warm thanks to my collaborator on the Mextasy.tv project (producer/director Miguel-Angel Soria), for sharing with me this latest incarnation of made-to-order, er maid-to-order, "Mexican" marionettes.

6. https://en.wikipedia.org/wiki/Erik_Estrada. Of course, Wikipedia is only the beginning of a veritable plethora of Estrada-focused volumes. True students of Estrada, an eighties TV Olivier of sorts, are urged to consult Estrada's *Erik Estrada: My Road from Harlem to Hollywood.*

7. The IMDB page is clear to be a tad dubious about this content—still I think it is priceless: "The content of this page was created by users. It has not been screened or verified by IMDB staff. Warning! This character biography may contain plot spoilers."

8. Source: http://web.archive.org/web/20161113220912/http://www.imdb.com/character/ch0037587/bio.

9. Ferguson, "Dax Shepard and Michael Peña Explain Why 'CHIPS' Needed to Be a Movie (Sort Of)."

10. Molina-Guzmán, *Latinas and Latinos on TV,* 9.

11. Blake and Ábrego, "An Interview with Gloria Anzaldúa."

12. Molina-Guzmán, *Latinas and Latinos on TV,* 33–34.

13. Baldwin, *Notes of a Native Son,* 94.

14. Baldwin, *Notes of a Native Son,* 111.

15. As this book was going to press, the episode was still available here: http://www.dailymotion.com/video/x2oah09 (accessed December 9, 2017).

16. Wikipedia, "List of ChiPs Episodes."

17. "*CHiPs,* 'Disaster Squad.'"

18. Here again one has to be a neo-eugenicist to track the bleaching of outsized Latina/o stereotypes in Hollywood movies. You might think, "Aha! Pacino, gone! Good!" Replaced by a Latino, but Bratt's not the Latino/a that most American audiences would recognize. Take it away, Wikipedia: "Bratt was born in San Francisco, California, the son of Eldy (*née* Banda), a nurse, and Peter Bratt Sr., a sheet metal worker. His mother is an indigenous activist of the Quechua ethnic group; born in Peru, and moved to the United States at age 14.[3] His father was American and had Austrian, English, and German ancestry" (Wikipedia, "Benjamin Bratt").

19. Douglas Harper's "Online Etymological Dictionary" is to the point: "relegate (v.) 1590s 'to banish, send into exile,' from Latin *relegatus*, past participle of *relegare* 'remove, dismiss, banish, send away, schedule, put aside,' from *re-*'back' (see *re-*) + *legare* 'send with a commission' (see *legate*). Meaning 'place in a position of inferiority' is recorded from 1790."
20. Source: http://eyegiene.sdsu.edu/2007/spring/e725/ (accessed May 21, 2017).
21. Online Etymology Dictionary, s.v. "obscene (adj.)."
22. I am in debt to Fede Aldama for the inspiration that led to this graphic—it was his invitation to lecture and exhibit *Mextasy* at The Ohio State University that gave birth to this allegorical trifle.
23. Diaz, "Los Lobos: Kiko."
24. Roberts, "Five Videos That Prove Los Lobos Has Earned a Rock and Roll Hall of Fame Nod."
25. Morris, *Los Lobos: Dream in Blue*, 116.

Notes to Section III

1. Nericcio and García-Martínez, "Superman Saves the Barrio for the United Farmworkers Union!"
2. Wikipedia, "List of *Wonder Woman* Episodes."
3. Américo Paredes's monograph *With His Pistol in His Hand: A Border Ballad* is a foundational text along with Gloria Anzaldúa and Cherríe Moraga's anthology, *This Bridge Called My Back*. Without these two works, American Studies, Cultural Studies, Ethnic Studies would not exist as we know them.
4. "The High Chaparral: Manolito Montoya."
5. Pippins and Delgado, *Henry Darrow: Lightning in the Bottle*. Quotation from https://www.henrydarrowbook.com//bookreviews.html.
6. Chee, "Science Fiction in Latino Studies Today . . . and in the Future," 116.
7. Chee, "Science Fiction in Latino Studies Today . . . and in the Future," 116.
8. Chee, "Science Fiction in Latino Studies Today . . . and in the Future," 117.
9. Frew, "Wilson Cruz Opens Up about 'Star Trek' Finally Going Gay."
10. Ramírez, "Afrofuturism/Chicanafuturism: Fictive Kin," 185.
11. Ramírez, "Afrofuturism/Chicanafuturism: Fictive Kin," 185–86.
12. One of the best essays to explore the nexus of capital, frontiers, the erotic, and border economies is Josefina Saldaña's outrageously nuanced meditation on NAFTA and Alfonso Cuarón's *Y Tu Mamá También*—her conclusion is as overwhelming as it is illuminating, setting the table as it were, for Rivera's dystopic science fiction film: "The border patrols increased, militarized presence along the Southwest border drives immigrants into the most lethal terrain under the pretext of national security. There, they will meet with vigilante citizen groups, legally armed and ready to perform 'citizens' arrests' of these undocumented immigrants. If these immigrants are lucky, they will be turned over to the border patrol unharmed for deportation. If they are even luckier, they will meet members of other citizen groups, armed with only a liberal discourse of human rights, who will provide food, shelter, water, and medical care, so that these immigrants may proceed to

enter the legal borderland of undocumented status, where they remain and yet somehow stay away." Saldaña-Portillo, "In the Shadow of NAFTA," 777.

13. Aldama, "Toward a *Transfrontera*-LatinX Aesthetic."
14. Schreiber, "The Undocumented Everyday," 306.
15. Bill Koenig, summary of *Dragnet 1967,* "The Christmas Story," IMDb, http://www.imdb.com/title/tt0565669/plotsummary?ref_=tt_ov_pl (accessed June 12, 2017).
16. See Chiu; McGee and Owens.
17. See an update to this news story: https://www.wsaz.com/content/news/Naya-Rivera-arrested-in-Kanawha-County-460016423.html.
18. Harper, *Online Etymological Dictionary,* s.v. "Manichaeism."

Notes to Section IV

1. "Hungry Muppet."
2. Kelsen, "Why Hollywood Can't Put Real-Life Mexicans on TV."
3. https://www.rottentomatoes.com/m/the_curse_of_la_llorona_2019

Notes to Section V

1. Chavez, *The Latino Threat,* 3.
2. Wikipedia, "Lou Dobbs."
3. Bebout, *Whiteness on the Border,* 31.
4. Fojas, "Border Media and New Spaces of Latinidad," 41.
5. Knowles, "Bordertown: Laredo: TV Review."
6. *"Bordertown: Laredo,* 'The Candyman.'"
7. "Al Roker Entertainment Presents Bordertown: Laredo (A&E)."
8. Rashotte, "Narco Cultura," 395.
9. Sanchez, "Smuggling as a Spectacle," 414.
10. Jason de León, https://lsa.umich.edu/anthro/people/faculty/socio-cultural-faculty/jpdeleon.html.
11. Shumaker, "On Those Who Live and Die along the Border."
12. "Director Alejandro González Iñárritu's Virtual Film Takes Us Inside a Dangerous Border Crossing."
13. "Q&A—Raymond Cruz (Tuco)."
14. González, "Intertextploitation and Post-Post-Latinidad in *Planet Terror,*" 124.
15. *"The Doris Day Show,* 'The Friend.'"
16. *"The Doris Day Show,* "The Friend, Plot."
17. I am indebted to my dear friend Professor Michael Wyatt Harper, Mount San Antonio College, Walnut, California, for bringing this epic episode to my attention.

Notes to Coda

1. Audrya Flores, "Take Care" and "Reanimate."

2. One of the first entries that came up with a Google search of the term "Hot Latina."

3. William Nericcio, "Alfonso Cuarón's *Children of Men*: Dystopic Cinema on the Verge or A Film of Revelation," for LASER and the Department of English @ OSU, The Ohio State University, March 8, 2017.

4. Desta, "*I Love Dick* Breakout Roberta Colindrez Is Raising Eyebrows and Breaking Barriers."

5. Deeb, "Ethnic Dispute Brews over Prinze's 'Chico.'"

6. This quote is drawn from https://en.wikipedia.org/wiki/Pilsen_Historic_District—however, accessed December 10, 2017; for a deeper, more evocative record of Mexican and other ethnic bodies in the Pilsen district, seek out Ramirez et al., *Chicanas of 18th Street: Narratives of a Movement from Latino Chicago.*

7. Rabin, "Louie: 'Dad.'"

8. Rabin, "Louie: 'Dad.'"

9. Wikipedia, "Louis C.K." If you can take it, listen to Louis C.K. lay out his background in this awful, offensive radio show—the hosts, New York City–based Opie and Anthony of *The Opie and Anthony Show,* joke about how Louis is a "spic" not a "mick," and other assorted feats of spoken ugliness—with a joke or two: "Louis CK Explains . . . His Origin."

10. Jones, "A Timeline of the Louis C.K. Masturbation Allegations."

11. Rodriguez, *Days of Obligation,* xv.

12. Rodriguez, *Days of Obligation,* 106.

BIBLIOGRAPHY

"Al Roker Entertainment Presents Bordertown: Laredo (A&E)." June 18, 2012. https://www.youtube.com/watch?v=youZUbZaNUc (accessed June 5, 2017).

Aldama, Frederick Luis. *The Adventures of Chupacabra Charlie.* Columbus: OSU Press, 2020.

———. "Robert Rodriguez's Fever-Dream: *Alita* and the Building of Latinx Sci-Fi Worlds." *Latinx Spaces*, February 22, 2019. https://www.latinxspaces.com/latinx-film/robert-rodriguez-fever-dream-alita-and-the-building-of-latinx-sci-fi-worlds.

———. *Latinx Superheroes in Mainstream Comics.* Tucson: University of Arizona Press, 2017.

———. "Toward a Transfrontera-Latinx Aesthetic: An Interview with Filmmaker Alex Rivera." *Latino Studies*, vol. 15, no. 3, 2017: 373–80.

Anonymous. "Film Box Office Wrap for the Weekend of April 10–12." *Daily Variety*, vol. 303, no. 6, Tuesday April 14, 2009: 5.

Anzaldúa, Gloria, and Cherrie Moraga. *This Bridge Called My Back: Writings By Radical Women of Color.* Watertown, MA: Persephone Press, 1981.

Aparicio, Frances, and Susana Chávez-Silverman, eds. *Tropicalizations: Transcultural Representations of Latinidad.* Hanover, NH: University Press of New England, 1997.

Baldwin, James. "The American Dream and the American Negro." *New York Times*, March 7, 1965. https://archive.nytimes.com/www.nytimes.com/books/98/03/29/specials/baldwin-dream.html.

———. *Notes of a Native Son.* New York: Beacon Press, 2012.

Baudrillard, Jean. *Simulations.* Translated by Phil Beitchman et al., New York: Semiotext(e), 1983.

Bebout, Lee. *Whiteness on the Border: Mapping the U.S. Racial Imagination in Brown and White.* New York: New York University Press, 2016.

Begley, Sarah. "Sofia Vergara Was Literally Put on a Pedestal in a Completely Sexist Bit at the Emmys." *Time*, August 26, 2014, http://time.com/3179558/2014-emmys-sofia-vergara/ (accessed June 7, 2017).

Beltrán, Mary. *Latina/o Stars in U.S. Eyes: The Making and Meanings of Film and TV Stardom.* Urbana: University of Illinois Press, 2009.

Berger, John. *Ways of Seeing.* London: Penguin, 2008; originally published in 1972.

Blake, Debbie and Carmen Ábrego, "An Interview with Gloria Anzaldúa." *Iowa Journal of Cultural Studies* (1995): 12–22. https://ir.uiowa.edu/ijcs/vol1995/iss14/3 (accessed December 8, 2017).

"*Bordertown: Laredo,* "The Candyman." IMDb, 2011. https://www.imdb.com/title/tt2796184/plotsummary?ref_=tt_ov_pl. (accessed June 5, 2017).

Bradshaw, Kelsey. "Texas Roadhouse Employee Fired after Tweeting She Would 'Kill as Many Mexicans' as Possible." *mySA,* July 25, 2016, https://www.mysanantonio.com/news/local/article/Texas-Roadhouse-employee-fired-after-tweeting-she-8406885.php#photo-10639301.

Chavez, Leo R. *The Latino Threat: Constructing Immigrants, Citizens, and the Nation.* Stanford, CA: Stanford University Press, 2013.

Chee, Fabio. "Science Fiction in Latino Studies Today . . . and in the Future." In *The Routledge Companion to Latino/a Pop Culture,* edited by Frederick Luis Aldama, 110–19. New York: Routledge, 2016.

"*CHiPs,* 'Disaster Squad.'" IMDb, https://www.imdb.com/title/tt0534446/.

Chiu, Melody. "Naya Rivera Charged with Domestic Battery After Alleged Altercation with Husband Ryan Dorsey." *People,* November 26, 2017. http://people.com/tv/naya-rivera-arrested-west-virginia/ (accessed December 9, 2017).

"Coco." *Box Office Mojo,* n.d. https://www.boxofficemojo.com/movies/?page=weekly&id=pixar1117.htm.

Dávila, Arlene. *Latinos, Inc.: The Marketing and Making of a People.* Berkeley: University of California Press, 2001.

De León, Jason. *The Land of Open Graves: Living and Dying on the Migrant Trail.* Berkeley, CA: University of California Press, 2015.

Deeb, Gary. "Ethnic Dispute Brews over Prinze's 'Chico.'" *Chicago Tribune,* October 4, 1974. http://archives.chicagotribune.com/1974/10/04/page/25/article/ethnic-dispute-brews-over-prinze-s-chico (accessed June 6, 2017).

Desta, Yohana. "*I Love Dick* Breakout Roberta Colindrez Is Raising Eyebrows and Breaking Barriers: The Actress Talks Playing a Sexually Fluid Artist in Amazon's Fascinating Series." *Vanity Fair,* May 12, 2017 https://www.vanityfair.com/hollywood/2017/05/roberta-colindrez-i-love-dick (accessed December 9, 2017).

Diaz, Cesar. "Los Lobos: Kiko." *Pop Matters,* March 9, 2004. http://www.popmatters.com/review/loslobos-kikos/ (accessed June 9, 2017).

"Director Alejandro González Iñárritu's Virtual Film Takes Us Inside a Dangerous Border Crossing." *NBC News,* May 22, 2017. https://www.nbcnews.com/news/latino/director-alejandro-gonzalez-inarritus-virtual-film-takes-us-inside-dangerous-n762866.

Dorfman, Ariel, and Armand Mattelart. *Para Leer El Pato Donald.* Coyocan, Mexico and Buenos Aires, Argentina: Siglo Veintiuno Editores, 1972.

"*The Doris Day Show,* 'The Friend.'" 1968. IMDb. https://www.imdb.com/title/tt1044266/ (accessed January 4, 2018).

"The Doris Day Show, 'The Friend,' Plot." 1968. IMDb. http://www.imdb.com/title/
tt1044266/plotsummary?ref_=tt_ov_pl (accessed January 4, 2018).

Egner, Jeremy. "'Ozark' on Netflix: This Lake Has Hidden Depths." *New York Times*,
July 14, 2017. https://www.nytimes.com/2017/07/14/arts/television/ozark-
netflix-jason-bateman-laura-linney.html.

Estrada, Erik. *Erik Estrada: My Road from Harlem to Hollywood*. Written with Davin
Seay. New York: William Morrow & Co, 1997.

Federal Communications Commission. *Hispanic Television Study*. Washington, DC:
Office of Strategic Planning and Policy Analysis and Industry Analysis Division,
Media Bureau, May 2016.

Ferguson, Latoya. "Dax Shepard and Michael Peña Explain Why 'CHIPS' Needed
to Be a Movie (Sort Of)." *Uproxx*, March 22, 2017, http://uproxx.com/movies/
chips-interview-michael-pena-dax-shepard/ (accessed May 20, 2017).

Fernández L'Hoeste, Héctor D. *Lalo Alcaraz: Political Cartooning in the Latino
Community*. Jackson: University Press of Mississippi, 2017.

Flores, Audrya. "Take Care" (https://jaguar-opossum.blogspot.com/2016/07/take-
care.html) and "Reanimate" (https://jaguar-opossum.blogspot.com/2016/11/
reanimate.html).

Fojas, Camilla. *Border Bandits: Hollywood on the Southern Frontier*. Austin: University of
Texas Press, 2008.

———. "Border Media and New Spaces of Latinidad." In *Latinos and Narrative Media:
Participation and Portrayal*, edited by Frederick Luis Aldama, 35–47. New York:
Palgrave Macmillan, 2013.

Fregoso, Rosa Linda. *The Bronze Screen: Chicana and Chicano Film Culture*. Minneapolis:
University of Minnesota Press, 1993.

Frew, James. "Wilson Cruz Opens Up about 'Star Trek' Finally Going Gay." Huffington
Post, October 26, 2016. https://www.huffingtonpost.com/entry/wilson-cruz-
opens-up-about-star-trek-finally-going_us_59f27f19e4b06ae9067ab79b (accessed
December 9, 2017).

Fuentes, Carlos. *The Buried Mirror: Reflections on Spain and the New World*. New York:
Mariner Books, 1992.

González, Christopher. "Intertextploitation and Post-Post-Latinidad in *Planet Terror*."
In Critical Approaches to the Films of Robert Rodriguez, edited by Frederick Luis
Aldama, 121–40. Austin: University of Texas Press, 2015.

González, Christopher, and Frederick Luis Aldama. *Graphic Borders: Latino Comic Books
Past, Present, and Future*. Austin: University of Texas Press, 2016.

Harper, Douglas. *Online Etymological Dictionary*, s.v. "Manichaeism." https://www.
etymonline.com/word/manichaeism (accessed December 9, 2017).

Hernandez, G. *Birdland*. Seattle: Eros Comix, 1990–1991.

———. *Blubber*. Issues 1–4. 2015–2017.

———. *Garden of the Flesh*. Seattle: Fantagraphics, 2016.

"The High Chaparral: Manolito Montoya." *The High Chaparral*, http://www.
thehighchaparral.com/chara1d.htm (accessed May 29, 2017).

"Hungry Muppet to Appear on 'Sesame Street.'" *CBS News,* October 7, 2011. http://www.cbsnews.com/news/hungry-muppet-to-appear-on-sesame-street/ (accessed June 2, 2017).

Jones, Nate. "A Timeline of the Louis C.K. Masturbation Allegations." *Vulture,* November 9, 2017. https://www.vulture.com/2017/11/louis-c-k-masturbation-allegations-a-timeline.html.

Kafka, Franz. *Metamorphosis.* Translated by Susan Bernofsky. New York: Norton, 2014.

Kelsen, David. "Why Hollywood Can't Put Real-Life Mexicans on TV." *OC Weekly,* May 25, 2016. http://www.ocweekly.com/film/why-hollywood-cant-put-real-life-mexicans-on-tv-7210730 (accessed June 3, 2017).

Kerouac, Jack. *On the Road.* New York: Viking. 1957.

Knowles, David. "Bordertown: Laredo: TV Review." *The Hollywood Reporter,* October 12, 2011. https://www.hollywoodreporter.com/review/bordertown-laredo-tv-review-246310 (accessed June 5, 2017).

Lepore, Jill. *The Secret History of Wonder Woman.* New York: Knopf, 2014.

"The Man Who Is Manolito! An Interview with Harry Darrow." *Henry's Western Roundup,* January 13, 2013. http://henryswesternroundup.blogspot.com/2013/01/the-man-who-is-manolito.html.

Mastro, Dana E., and Elizabeth Behm-Morawitz. "Latino Representation on Primetime Television." *Journalism & Mass Communication Quarterly,* vol. 82, no. 1, 2005: 110–30.

Mayer, Oliver. *Blade to the Heat.* New York: Dramatists Play Service, 1996.

McGee, Jatara, and Markie Owens. "Husband Says Actress Naya Rivera 'Is Out of Control' in 911 Call after Domestic Battery Incident." *WSAZ,* November 28, 2017. http://www.wsaz.com/content/news/Naya-Rivera-arrested-in-Kanawha-County-460016423.html (accessed December 9, 2017).

———. "UPDATE: Domestic battery charge dropped against 'Glee' star." *WSAZ,* January 17, 2018. https://www.wsaz.com/content/news/Naya-Rivera-arrested-in-Kanawha-County-460016423.html (accessed May 10, 2019).

Mendible, Myra, ed. *From Bananas to Buttocks: The Latina Body in Popular Film and Culture.* Austin: University of Texas Press, 2007.

Miller, Arthur. *Death of a Salesman.* New York: Penguin Plays, 1976.

Molina-Guzmán, Isabel. *Dangerous Curves: Latina Bodies in the Media.* New York: New York University Press, 2010.

———. *Latinas and Latinos on TV: Colorblind Comedy in the Post-Racial Network Era.* Tucson: University of Arizona Press, 2018.

Morris, Chris. *Los Lobos: Dream in Blue.* Austin: University of Texas Press, 2015.

MPAA. Motion Picture Association of America report 2013. https://www.mpaa.org/wp-content/uploads/2014/03/MPAA-Theatrical-Market-Statistics-2013_032514-v2.pdf.

Negrón Muntaner, Frances. *Boricua Pop: Puerto Ricans and the Latinization of American Culture.* New York: New York University Press, 2004.

Nericcio, William. "Now You Can Insert 'Maria, the Maid' into Any Project You Dream Up!!!!" *Tex{t}-Mex Galleryblog*, November 6, 2014. http://textmex.blogspot.com/2014/11/now-you-can-insert-maria-maid-into-any.html.

Nericcio, William. *Tex[t]-Mex: Seductive Hallucinations of the "Mexican" in America*. Austin: University of Texas Press, 2007.

Nericcio, William, and Marc García-Martínez. "Superman Saves the Barrio for the United Farmworkers Union: Cesar Chavez's Buddy in Tights!" *Tex{t}-Mex Galleryblog*, October 8, 2009. http://textmex.blogspot.com/2007/09/superman-saves-barrio.html (accessed May 24, 2017).

Noriega, Chon, and Ana M. López, eds. *The Ethnic Eye: Latino Media Arts*. Minneapolis: University of Minnesota Press, c1996.

Online Etymology Dictionary, s.v. "obscene (adj.)." http://www.etymonline.com/index.php?term=obscene (accessed May 22, 2017).

"Opie & Anthony: Louis CK Explains . . . His Origin." jfoughe, September 28, 2009. https://www.youtube.com/watch?v=Ftf1VYHfsDg (accessed December 10, 2017).

Ovalle, Priscilla. *Dance and the Hollywood Latina: Race, Sex, and Stardom*. New Brunswick, NJ: Rutgers University Press, 2011.

Paredes, Américo. *With His Pistol in His Hand: A Border Ballad*. Austin: University of Texas Press, 1958.

Paredez, Deborah. *Selenidad: Selena, Latinos, and the Performance of Memory*. Durham, NC: Duke University Press, 2009.

Peretz, Evgenia. "Rose McGowan on Harvey Weinstein, Hollywood's Reckoning, and Writing Her New Memoir, BRAVE." *Vanity Fair*, January 3, 2018. https://www.vanityfair.com/hollywood/2018/01/rose-mcgowan-harvey-weinstein-hollywood-writing-memoir-brave (accessed January 4, 2018).

Pippins, Jan, and Henry Darrow Delgado. *Henry Darrow: Lightning in the Bottle*. Albany, GA: BearManor Media, 2015.

Plascencia, Salvador. *People of Paper*. San Francisco: McSweeney's Books, 2005.

"Q&A—Raymond Cruz (Tuco)." *AMC*, n.d. https://www.amc.com/shows/breaking-bad/talk/2009/03/raymond-cruz-interview.

Rabin, Nathan. "Louie: 'Dad.'" *AV/TV Club*, August 16, 2012. https://tv.avclub.com/louie-dad-1798173867 (accessed December 10, 2017).

Ramírez Berg, Charles. *Latino Images in Film: Stereotypes, Subversion, & Resistance*. Austin: University of Texas Press, 2002.

Ramírez, Catherine. "Afrofuturism/Chicanafuturism: Fictive Kin." *Aztlan: A Journal of Chicano Studies*, vol. 33, no. 1, 2008: 185–94.

Ramirez, Leonard G., with Yenelli Flores, Maria Gambo, Isaura González, Victoria Pérez, Magda Ramirez-Castañeda, and Cristina Vital. *Chicanas of 18th Street: Narratives of a Movement from Latino Chicago*. Latinos in Chicago and the Midwest. Chicago: University of Illinois Press, 2011.

Ramos, Jorge. *The Latino Wave: How Hispanics Are Transforming Politics in America*. New York: Harper Perennial, 2005.

Rashotte, Ryan. "Narco Cultura." In *The Routledge Companion to Latina/o Popular Culture,* edited by Frederick Luis Aldama, chap. 34. New York: Routledge, 2016.

Roberts, Randall. "Five Videos That Prove Los Lobos Has Earned a Rock and Roll Hall of Fame Nod." *Los Angeles Times,* October 8, 2005. http://www.latimes.com/entertainment/music/posts/la-et-ms-videos-los-lobos-rock-hall-of-fame-nod-20151008-story.html (accessed June 5, 2017).

Rodriguez, Richard. *Days of Obligation: An Argument with My Mexican Father.* New York: Penguin, 1992.

———. *Hunger of Memory: The Education of Richard Rodriguez: An Autobiography.* Boston: Godine, 1982.

Rodriguez, Richard T. *Next of Kin: The Family in Chicano/a Cultural Politics.* Durham, NC: Duke University Press, 2009.

Saldaña-Portillo, María Josefina. "In the Shadow of NAFTA: Y tu mamá también Revisits the National Allegory of Mexican Sovereignty." *American Quarterly,* vol. 57, no. 3 (2005): 751–77.

Sanchez, Gabriella. "Smuggling as a Spectacle: Irregular Migration and Coyotes in Contemporary US Latino Popular Culture." In *The Routledge Companion to Latina/o Popular Culture,* edited by Frederick Luis Aldama, chapter 35. New York: Routledge, 2016.

Sarduy, Severo. *Written on a Body,* translated by Carol Maier (New York: Lumen Books, 1989).

Schreiber, Rebecca. "The Undocumented Everyday: Migrant Rights and Visual Strategies in the work of Alex Rivera." *Journal of American Studies* vol. 50, no. 2 (2016): 305–27.

Shumaker, Jon M. "On Those Who Live and Die along the Border: Two New Books Look at the Ever-Changing Face of the U.S.-Mexico Border." *High Country News,* July 25, 2016. http://www.hcn.org/issues/48.12/on-those-who-live-and-die-along-the-border (accessed June 5, 2017).

Uffalussy, Jennifer Gerson. "Why Are Latino Viewers the Most Important for Networks?" *Guardian,* January 1, 2015. https://www.theguardian.com/tv-and-radio/tvandradioblog/2015/jan/01/why-are-latino-viewers-important-for-networks.

Valdes, Alicia. "Is Porn That Depicts the Subjugation of Hispanic Women Tied to the Rise of Hate Crimes Against Latinos?: Lou Dobbs Cheers on Anti-Latino Backlash, While Pornography Provides the Context for the Dangerous Stereotypes." *Alternet,* May 8, 2009. https://web.archive.org/web/20150807200417/http://www.alternet.org/story/139926/is_porn_that_depicts_the_subjugation_of_hispanic_women_tied_to_the_rise_of_hate_crimes_against_latinos.

Valdivia, Angharad N. *Latina/os and the Media.* Cambridge; Malden, MA: Polity Press, 2010.

Vargas, Andrew S. "5 Movie Roles That Made Lou Diamond Phillips an Honorary Latino." http://remezcla.com/film/tbt-5-film-roles-that-made-lou-diamond-phillips-an-honorary-latino/ (accessed May 20, 2017).

Wikipedia. "Benjamin Bratt." https://en.wikipedia.org/wiki/Benjamin_Bratt (accessed May 21, 2017).

Wikipedia. "Cristela." https://en.wikipedia.org/wiki/Cristela (accessed April 7, 2019).

Wikipedia. "List of *ChiPs* Episodes." https://en.wikipedia.org/wiki/List_of_CHiPs_episodes#Season_1:_1977.E2.80.9378 (accessed April 7, 2019).

Wikipedia. "List of *Wonder Woman* Episodes." https://en.wikipedia.org/wiki/List_of_Wonder_Woman_episodes (accessed April 7, 2019).

Wikipedia. "Lou Diamond Phillips." https://en.wikipedia.org/wiki/Lou_Diamond_Phillips (accessed May 20, 2017).

Wikipedia. "Lou Dobbs." https://en.wikipedia.org/wiki/Lou_Dobbs. (accessed April 7, 2019)

Wikipedia. "Louis C.K." https://en.wikipedia.org/wiki/Louis_C.K. (accessed December 10, 2017).

Wikipedia. "Lynda Carter." https://en.wikipedia.org/wiki/Lynda_Carter (accessed April 7, 2019).

Film

Arau, Sergio. *A Day Without a Mexican.* Altavista Films. 2004.

Ayala, Diego. *Conexión.* Azar Producciones. 2013.

Bobin, James. *Dora and the Lost City of Gold.* Paramount Players. 2019.

Cameron, Cody. *Cloudy with a Chance of Meatballs 2.* Sony Pictures Animation. 2013.

Campbell, Martin. *The Mask of Zorro.* Tristar Pictures. 1998.

Coffin, Pierre. *Despicable Me.* Universal Pictures. 2010.

———. *Despicable Me 2.* Universal Pictures. 2013.

Coppola, Sofia. *The Bling Ring.* American Zoetrope. 2013.

Cuarón, Alfonso. *Children of Men.* Universal Pictures. 2006.

———. *Y Tu Mamá Tambien.* 20th Century Fox. 2001.

De Palma, Brian. *Scarface.* Universal Pictures. 1983.

Docter, Pete. *Monsters, Inc.* Walt Disney Pictures, 2001.

Edwards, Gareth. *Monsters.* Vertigo Films. 2010.

Franklin, Carl. *Bless Me, Ultima.* Gran Via Productions. 2013.

Gilbert, Lewis. *Moonraker.* United Artists. 1979.

Gilroy, Dan. *Nightcrawler.* Bold Films. 2014

González Iñárritu, Alejandro. Legendary Entertainment. *Carne y Arena.* 2017.

Griffith, D. W. *Birth of a Nation.* David W. Griffith Corp. 1915.

Heineman, Matthew. *Cartel Land.* 2015.

Hess, Jared. *Nacho Libre.* Nickelodeon Movies. 2006.

Hill, Walter. *The Warriors*. Paramount Pictures. 1979.

Huston, John. *The Treasure of the Sierra Madre*. Warner Bros. 1948.

Kazan, Elia. *Viva Zapata!* 20th Century Fox. 1952.

Kubrick, Stanley. *Dr. Strangelove*. Columbia Pictures. 1964.

——. *2001: A Space Odyessey*. Metro-Goldwyn-Mayer, 1968.

Laresgoiti, Francisco. *2033*. Cinema Epoch. 2009.

Lasseter, John. *A Bug's Life*. Disney/Pixar. 1998.

——. *Toy Story 2*. Walt Disney Pictures, 1999.

——. *Cars*. Disney/Pixar. 2006.

——. *Cars 2*. Disney/Pixar. 2011.

Lin, Justin. *Fast & Furious*. Universal Pictures. 2009.

——. *Star Trek Beyond*. Paramount Pictures. 2016.

Lord, Phil. *Cloudy with a Chance of Meatballs*. Columbia Pictures. 2009.

Lucas, George. *Star Wars*. Lucasfilm Ltd. 1977.

Marín, Cheech. *Born in East LA*. Universal Pictures. 1987.

Martin, Darnell. *I Like It Like That*. Columbia Picture. 1994.

Meirelles, Fernando. *Blindness*. Focus & Miramax. 2008.

Menéndez, Ramón. *Stand and Deliver*. Warner Bros. 1988.

Miller, George. *Happy Feet 2*. Warner Bros. 2011.

Niblo, Fred. *Mark of Zorro*. United Artists. 1920.

Ordóñez Nischli, Rodrigo. *Depositarios*. De Cuernos Al Abismo. 2010.

Powell, Michael. *Peeping Tom*. Anglo-Amalgamated Film. 1960.

Richard Jones, F. *The Gaucho*. United Artists. 1927.

Ripoll, María. *Tortilla Soup*. Samuel Goldwyn Films. 2001.

Rivera, Alex. "A Robot Walks into a Bar." *YouTube,* uploaded by Futurestatestv, August 4, 2014. https://www.youtube.com/watch?v=fOz1cMu7hZQ.

——. *Sleep Dealer*. Maya Entertainment. 2008.

——. "Why Cybraceros?" *YouTube,* uploaded by Freewaves, December 3, 2012, https://www.youtube.com/watch?v=Xr1eqKcDZq4.

Rodriguez, Robert. *From Dusk till Dawn*. Miramax Films. 1996.

——. *Machete*. Troublemaker Studios. 2010.

——. *Machete Kills*. Troublemaker Studios. 2013.

——. *Planet Terror*. Troublemaker Studios. 2007.

——. *Spy Kids*. Dimension Films/Troublemaker Studios. 2001.

Salces, Carlos. *Zurdo*. Altavista Films. 2003.

Sapir, Esteban. *La antena*. Pachamama Cine. 2007.

Scorcese, Martin. *Gangs of New York*. Miramax. 2002.

Scott, Ridley. *Blade Runner*. Warner Bros. 1982.

Scribner, George. *Oliver & Company.* Disney Pictures. 1988.

Shepard, Dax. *CHiPS.* Warner Bros. 2017.

Snyder, Zachary. Snyder, Zach. *Man of Steel.* DC Entertainment. 2013.

———. *Batman v Superman: Dawn of Justice.* Warner Bros. 2016.

Soderbergh, Steven. *Sex, Lies, and Videotape.* Outlaw Productions. 1989.

———. *Contagion.* Warner Bros. 2011.

Soren, David. *Turbo.* Dreamworks. 2013.

Spielberg, Steven. *E.T. the Extra-Terrestrial.* Universal Pictures. 1982.

Stanton, Andrew. *Finding Nemo.* Walt Disney Productions. 2003.

Unkrich, Lee, and Adrian Molina. *Coco.* Disney/Pixar. 2017.

Valdez, Luis. *Zoot Suit.* Universal Pictures. 1981.

———. *La Bamba.* Columbia Pictures. 1987.

———. *Cisco and the Kid.* Turner Pictures. 1994.

Verbinksi, Gore. *Rango.* Nickelodeon Movies. 2011.

Villeneuve, Denis. *Blade Runner 2049.* Warner Bros. 2017.

Wang, Wayne. *Maid in Manhattan.* Columbia Pictures. 2002.

Welles, Orson. *Touch of Evil.* Universal Pictures. 1958.

Wilder, Billy. *Sunset Boulevard.* Paramount Pictures. 1950.

Wise, Robert. *Andromeda Strain.* Universal Pictures. 1971.

TV

13 Reasons Why. Netflix. 2017.

Addams Family. ABC. 1964–66.

Agents of S.H.I.E.L.D: Slingshot. ABC. 2016. http://abc.go.com/shows/marvels-agents-of-shield-slingshot. Accessed December 20, 2016.

All in the Family. CBS. 1971–79.

Barney & Friends. PBS. 1992–2010.

Batman. ABC. 1966–68.

Battlestar Galactica. ABC. 1978–79.

Battlestar Galactica. The Sci-Fi Channel. 2003–9.

Better Call Saul. AMC. 2015–.

Black Mirror. Channel 4. "Nosedive." Season 3, episode 1. October 2016.

Bonanza. NBC. 1959–73.

Border Patrol. National Geographic Channel. 2010–15.

Border Security: America's Frontline. GlobalTV. 2016–.

Border Wars. National Geographic Channel. 2010–15.

Bordertown. Fox. 2016.

Bordertown: Laredo. "The *Candyman.*" *dailymotion,* uploaded by Mackie33, 2015, http://www.dailymotion.com/video/x2ijxxw.

Breaking Bad. AMC. 2008–13.

Brooklyn Nine-Nine. Fox. 2013–.

Brujos. http://www.brujostv.com/

Caprica. SyFy. 2010.

El chapulin Colorado. 1972–81.

El Chavo del Ocho. Televisa. 1971–80.

Chico and the Man. NBC. 1974–78.

CHiPs. NBC. 1977–83.

Claws. TNT. 2017–.

Connections. BBC. 1978.

Cristela. ABC. 2014–15.

Devious Maids. ABC. 2013–16.

Dora the Explorer. Nickelodeon. 2000–14.

Dragnet. "The Christmas Story." Season 2, episode 15. NBC. December 21, 1967.

Drink, Slay, Love. Lifetime. 2017.

Dusk Till Dawn: The Series. El Rey Network. 2014–.

East WillyB. Web. http://www.eastwillyb.com/. 2011–.

El Tigre. Nickelodeon. 2007–8.

The Event. NBC. 2010–11.

Exorcist. Fox. 2017–.

Family Guy. Fox. 1999–.

The Flash. CW. 2014–.

Galactica. ABC. 1980.

George Lopez. ABC. 2002–7.

Gilligan's Island. CBS. 1964–67.

Glee. Fox. 2009–15.

Goliath. Amazon Studios. 2016–.

Good Times. CBS. 1974–79.

Handy Manny. Disney Junior. 2006–.

Happy Days. ABC. 1974–84.

The High Chapparal. NBC. 1967.

Homeland Security. USA. 2009.

I Love Dick. Amazon Studios. 2017.

I Love Lucy. CBS. 1951–57.

"I Luh Ya Papí." *YouTube,* uploaded by JenniferLopezVEVO, March 13, 2014, https://www.youtube.com/watch?v=c40iEhf9M04.

In Living Color. Fox. 1990–94.

Jane the Virgin. CW. 2014–.

Los Americans. "Season 1, episode 1 Preview." *YouTube,* uploaded by LosAmericans, May 26, 2011, https://www.youtube.com/watch?v=ANCS49kVUGE.

Lost in Space. CBS. 1965–68.

Louie. FX. 2010–2015.

Mad Men. AMC. 2007–15.

Maude. CBS. 1972–78.

Mextasy TV. http://www.mextasy.tv/.

Miami Vice. NBC. 1984–90.

Minoriteam. Adult Swim. 2005–6.

Modern Family. ABC. 2009–.

My So-Called Life. ABC. 1994–95.

My Three Sons. ABC then CBS. 1960–72.

Narcos. Netflix. 2015–.

The Office. NBC. 2005–13.

Orange Is the New Black. Netflix. 2013–.

Ozark. Netflix. 2017–.

The Powerpuff Girls. Cartoon Network. 1998–2005.

Queen of the South. Netflix. 2016–.

Sanford and Son. NBC. 1972–77.

Scrubs. NBC; ABC. 2001–10.

Sesame Street. PBS. 1969–.

Shades of Blue. NBC. 2016–18.

Siempre en Domingo. Televisa. 1969–98.

"Speedy Gonzales." *Looney Tunes.* Warner Brothers. 1953–2015.

Star Trek: Discovery. CBS. 2017–.

Supergirl. CBS. 2015–.

Scrubs. ABC and NBC. 2001–10.

The Simpsons. Fox. 1989–.

The Sopranos. HBO Entertainment. 1999–2007.

The Super Friends. "Alien Mummy." Season 6, episode 6. ABC. October 1981.

True Blood. HBO. 2008–14.

Underworld Inc. National Geographic. 2015.

The Walking Dead. AMC. 2010–.

Westworld. HBO. 2017–.

Whirligig. 1950–56, BBC. https://en.wikipedia.org/wiki/Whirligig_(TV_series).

Wonder Woman. CBS. 1975–79.

Z Nation. SyFy. 2017–.

Desperate Housewives, 28, 86

Despicable Me, 41

Despicable Me 2, 41

Despositarios, 79

Devious Maids, 7, 10, 27

Día de los Muertos facepaint, 58

Diamond Phillips, Lou, 27

Diaz, Cesar, 48

Díaz, Junot, 139

Diehl, John, 84

Disney, 41, 43, 76, 85, 101

Dobbs, Lou, 110–13, 117

Donnelly, Eddie, 92

Dora and the Lost City of Gold, 94

Dora the Explorer: Into the City (game), 94; TV show, 91, 94–95, 99

Dorfman, Ariel, 41

Doris Day Show, The, 128–30

Downey Jr., Robert, 127

Dr. Strangelove, 126

Dragnet, 84–85

Drink, Slay, Love, 155

drones (Alex Rivera), 80

Dubuque, Bill, 27

Dunn, John, 17–19

"East Coast Latinx Gravity" 38

East Los High, 104

East WillyB, 3, 38

Edwards, Gareth, 119

El Chapo, 104

El Chapulín Colorado, 92–93, 102, 106

El Chavo del Ocho, 96

El Dorado, 5, 90–91

"El Hielo (ICE)" music video, 81–82

El Murciélago Negro!, 56

El Tigre: The Adventures of Manny Rivera, 5, 95

Elizondo, Héctor, 107

Equihua, Sandra, 95

erasure, 4, 149

Espinosa, Carla, 34

Esposito Alessandro, Giancarlo Giuseppe, 40

Estrada, Erik, 30, 33, 36–38

Estudiante, Julio, 102

E.T. the Extra-Terrestrial, 74–75

Ethnic Eye, The, 6

Event, The, 77

Exorcist (TV show), 114

Eyegasm (age of), 21

Eyegiene (age of), 21

Fairbanks, Douglas, 42, 53

Fajardo, Kat, 139

Family Guy, 103

Fast & Furious, 22

Fernández L'Hoeste, Héctor D., 136

Ferrell, Will, 41

Fiennes, Ralph, 28

Finding Nemo, 43

Flash, The, 127

Flores, Audrya, 140–42

Fojas, Camilla, 6, 113

Fonz, The, 30, 100

food, 105–8

Ford, Harrison, 75

Fox Business Network, 112

Foxx, Redd, 12, 16

Franklin, Carl, 124

Fregoso, Rosa Linda, 6

Freleng, Friz, 17–20

Freleng, Isadore "Yitzak" "Friz," 97

From Bananas to Buttocks, 5

From Dusk till Dawn, 122

Froom, Mitch, 48–49

Fuentes, Carlos, 9

Librotraficante, 137

Lima, Anglo Floriana, 128

Limbaugh, Rush, 110, 113

Lin, Justin, 22

Lincoln, Andrew, 122

Loman, Willy, 11

Longoria, Eva, 5, 7, 9–10, 27–86, 104

Lopez, Alma, 139

López, Ana M., 6

Lopez, George, 151

Lopez, Jennifer, 27–28, 45, 81,

López Mercado, Ana, 146

Los Americans, 107, 109

Los Bros Hernandez, 137

Los Lobos: Dream in Blue, 50

Los Lobos, 48–49, 51

Lost in Space, 25

Lou Dobbs Tonight, 110–12

Louie, 152–54

Louis C.K., 151–55

Lovato, Demi, 13, 85

Love & Rockets, 100, 137

"Lowdrone" installment, 79

Lubezki, Emmanuel, 146

Lucas, George, 126

lucha libre, 93

luchadores, 56

Luna, Diego, 146

Machete, 13–15, 53, 87, 125, 14

Machete Kills, 125–26, 143

Mad Men, 38

Madera, Hemky, 43

Maid in Manhattan, 28

mainstream media, 6, 114

mamás (on TV), 28, 68, 84, 86,

Man of Steel, 59

Fuller, Bryan, 73

Fumero, Melissa, 32–33

Galactica (1980), 71

gangbanger (stereotype). See Latinx gangbanger

Gangs of New York, 133

García Bernal, Gael, 43, 104

García-Martinez, Marc, 57

García-Rulfo, Manuel, 124

Garden of the Flesh, 138

Gaucho, The, 42, 65

George Lopez, 7, 17, 106

Gershwin, Gina, 122

Gilb, Dagoberto, 137

Gilbert, Lewis, 126

Gilligan, Vince, 38

Gilligan's Island, 25

Gilroy, Dan, 36

Glee, 86

Godot, Gal, 62

Golden Age of Television, The, 38, 104

Goliath, 124

Gomez, Selena, 85, 148

Gomez Bolaños, Roberto, 92

González, Christopher, 125

Gonzalez Gonzalez, Pedro, 77

Good Times, 71

Goodman, Dana Min, 151, 153

Gosling, Ryan, 76

Goyer, David, 59

Graphic Borders, 137–38

greaser: films, 13; stereotype, 100, 148

Greenaway, Peter, 51

Griffith, D. W., 52–53, 65, 96, 122

Guerrero, Diane, 35

Gugliemi, Noel, 122

Gurba, Myriam, 33, 135

Gustin, Grant, 127

Gutierrez, Jorge R., 95

Gyllenhaal, Jake, 36

Handy Manny, 43, 94

Hannity, Sean, 112

Happy Days, 30, 100

Happy Feet 2, 41–42

Hardy, Tom, 59

Hastings, Reed, 114

Hauer, Rutger, 75

Hayek, Salma, 90, 122

Hayworth, Rita, 48, 90

Heath, Stephen, 53

Heckle and Jeckle, 92

Heineman, Matthew, 114

Hernandez, Gilbert, 144

Hernandez, Jaime, 100

Hernandez, Marisol "La Marisoul," 81

Herrera, Alfonso, 115

Hess, Jerrod, 5, 93

Hessler, Gordon, 36

Heston, Charlton, 40, 90

High Chaparral, The, 23, 64, 69

hipster porn (concept), 146

hipster racism, 108

Hodge, Max, 36

Holland, Tom, 19

Holloway, Elizabeth, 63

Hollywood Reporter, The, 113

Homeland Security: USA, 5, 113

Hopkins, Anthony, 76

hot-blooded Latina (stereotype), 42, 56

Huston, John, 65

hypersexualization, 4, 6–7, 32, 42, 45–47, 86, 99, 142–43, 154

I/Eye Eva, 47–48

I Am Not Your Negro, 134

I Like It Like That, 45

I Love Dick, 148

ICE, 81

In Living Color, 28

Iñárritu, Alejandro (

internalized colonia

Iron Man, 127

Isaacs, Jason, 74

Jack Benny Program,

Jane the Virgin, 13, 1(

Jennings, John, 139

Jimenez, Hector, 93

Johns, Geoff, 127

Johnson, Bruce, 128

Johnson, Don, 84

Joker, The, 59–60

Jones, Rashida, 79

Joy, Lisa, 77

Justice League of Ame

Kafka, Franz, 11

Kane, Bob, 56

Katz, Evan, 77

Kerouac, Jack, 119

Kiko, 48–49

Kirkland, Mark, 101

Knowles, David, 11?

Koenig, Bill, 84–85

Kreisberg, Andrew, :

Kubrick, Stanley, 12(

Kurtzman, Alex, 73

Kurtzman, Robert, 1

La antena, 79

La Bamba, 27, 72

la llorona, 104–5

la malinche, 84

La reina del sur, 114